WHAT'S IN A NAME?

Why pay more for a well-advertised eye shadow, a miracle moisturizer, or a high-fashion facial when you can get the same thing at half the price?

Judi McMahon shows you how to cut through the glamorous wrappings and get down to basics. Discover the low-cost way to keep your hair, skin, nails, and figure looking fabulous. Learn how to read between the lines of labels . . . how to buy and apply inexpensive substitutes . . . how to make home products for mere pennies.

You can learn the secrets that let you double your beauty budget. Start saving your money and . . .

LOOK SUPER FOR LESS

LOOK SUPER FOR LESS

Judi McMahon

A DELL BOOK

To Baba Muktananda with love,
who has given me every golden opportuni
and immense rewards along the way,
jai gurudev.

Published by
Dell Publishing Co., Inc.
1 Dag Hammarskjold Plaza
New York, New York 10017

Dell ® TM 681510, Dell Publishing Co., Inc.

ISBN: 0-440-14904-5

Printed in the United States of America

First printing—November 1981

ACKNOWLEDGMENTS

To the physicians who furnished me with facts, and enhanced this guide, my grateful thanks. To Connie Clausen, whose idea it was, my deepest appreciation.

To Coleen O'Shea, my editor, my special gratefulness for her patience and pleasantness and professionalism.

To Caroline Penna, marketing director of Andrea Products, to Yolanda Lazo of Maybelline and to Helen Nash for Noxzema and Cover Girl for information, my warm thanks. To Helen Oppenheim of Vidal Sassoon, for her knowledgeable help and superb direction on hairstyling and trends; to makeup artists Ted Nadel, Bevy Chase, and Raphael Tosta; to hair colorist extraordinary, Edward Moore of Vidal Sassoon for his special formulas and information, my eternal thanks.

To James Fahnestock for his good-looking illustrations and soft and patient manner, and to Maureen McMahon and Sunny Carmell for researching product information, my thanks as well.

And, to all the unsung heroines, the audience of women out there, who inspired me with the need to say, yes, you can look beautiful, feel better, and, stay younger looking longer, without having to go broke in the process, thank you, thank you.

TABLE OF CONTENTS

The tips in this book have all worked for different women. However, everyone is an individual, and not all tips will be suitable for you. If you have any question at all about allergies or any medical contraindications, please check with your doctor for approval before use. The author and publisher advise you to use care, common sense, and your knowledge of yourself when using these products and preparing these recipes.

FOREWORD

In this book Judi McMahon has taken a practical philosophy and translated it into a simple, easy-to-read beauty guidebook for all women. Applying her own experiences in the field of self-improvement and beauty, Ms. McMahon has come up with reasonable, commonsense alternatives and effective ways of achieving them. And to her credit, she does it by always keeping a woman's budget in mind.

As a plastic surgeon I often see women who seek redress from scars, serious skin growths, as well as the effects and damages of premature aging. Everything from hyperpigmentation of the skin to unsightly scars that are the residue of severe acne, to age spots and deep lines and wrinkles, are conditions with which I must deal on an everyday basis in my medical practice.

Often many of the women who consult with me mention their having spent many years experimenting with various and sundry facial creams and lotions and of spending great sums of money in the hope of help and alleviation. Some mistakenly, seeking instant solutions to their skin and beauty problems, have sought out not-so-honest facial experts. Unfortunately many of the remedies they are given are damaging to the skin, or at the least, ineffectual—a waste of time and money. For in truth the same cream that is touted as a restorer or regenerator of cells, that is packaged elegantly and sold at upward of a hundred dollars an ounce, can be found in nearly the same formula in a plain package at the local store.

In my considered professional opinion no beauty product now on the market can serve as that magic elixir. Skin type, nutrition, life-style, the genetic factor—all of these facets play a part in the basic skin texture and appearance and in how a woman will age.

Women are by nature realistic. Learn to be realistic about your appearance: your hair, your skin, your face and body. If you find you do have a recurring problem, a degenerating condition that no cream or lotion can help, then by all means consult with a physician. Similarly, avail yourself of the latest factual information; learn how to apply the best commonsense skin- and hair-care tips, like those given to you in this guide. In this manner you will no longer be susceptible to becoming another vulnerable victim; you will avoid overpaying to enter the world of beauty.

It wasn't until 1977 that the FDA finally required manufacturers to list the ingredients on their cosmetic packages. Still, the labels won't tell you all you need to know about a particular ingredient or preservative listed on a label. Remember: Becoming an aware consumer will help you to take the best possible care of you that you can.

That is why I welcome a book of this kind. This guide avoids the fads in color, style, and fashion. It doesn't promise you eternal youth or beauty. It is a commonsense handbook by a woman for all women. It says you don't have to spend your hard-earned money on overadvertised and overpriced products. That you can apply some basic rules and learn an intelligent approach to finding far less expensive products and treatments that really achieve the same results and, in some cases, better ones.

Jane N. Haher, M.D.
St. Vincent's Hospital
New York City

CHAPTER 1

Beauty on a Budget

Why I Wrote This Book

Elizabeth Taylor. Greta Garbo. Marilyn Monroe. Sophia Loren. Merle Oberon. All those dazzling cinema queens. My, oh my, how I looked up to them with admiration, wondering if I could ever be as beautiful; if my hair could look as shiny and touchable; if I could wear my lashes as long and lipstick as lustfully, so that *he* would find me.

Would love indeed find its way to my door? Would beauty find me? Was I as pretty, as kissable, as all those lovely ladies on the silver screen? And then there were all those ads I grew up and thrived upon—all the cover girls mouthing slogans in my favorite magazines saying I too could look just as fabulous! If only I would use the same brand and color, if only I was willing to spend that outrageous sum for that super-duper cream those seductive ads said would make it all perfect, would make me look like a million dollars. But only if I was willing to throw out last season's eyeshadow color and update it for the manufacturer's new look. After all, didn't I want to be *au courant?* Wasn't

I willing to pay for it? To spend. And spend. And spend.

Those were the days, my friends. Thank heaven they're gone. Like most of us I've grown up, finally, and have become a wise and wary consumer. Somehow I grew sensible enough to learn that, no, one needn't buy that balmy royal bee balm at ninety-five dollars an ounce to look like those movie heroines. And nonsense to all those placenta emollients and extravagantly praised deep-pore potions and oil of ermine creams that were really just a lot of wasted effort. Now that I was armed with the facts, I could do just as well—no, better—with inexpensive products and even with some of those I could make up for myself.

For, in truth, you *can* find a million-dollar face in the five-and-ten-cent store. And, honestly, you don't have to spend a fortune to be beautiful. It's not money you have to spend. It's time. And attention. For beauty is all in the application. And so this book. For as a concerned woman, and as a beauty editor, I have spent the last decade learning all I can about the cosmetic and aligned skin- and hair-care industries. I have taken the time to try out every conceivable product, technique, and method offered, expensive or not. I have found out for myself what works and what doesn't. And now I can share with all of you how you can save money and get results.

What This Guide Contains

I have taken the tips I have learned from the experts, as well as those tricks and helpful hints I have adapted for myself, and have compiled the best of them. I have gathered the latest makeup know-how and product research and discovered what products you can find at the discount and dime and chain stores and have put all of this information together into this one compact, money-saving beauty guide.

Many perfectly fine cosmetics are discounted for reasons that have nothing to do with quality. Some cosmetics are brought out and targeted for a market that turns out not to be salable and so they end up in the chain and discount counters. Perfectly good makeup sold under celebrity names bomb and also end up on sale at fifty percent and more off in the local chain and variety stores. And so you'll also do well to shop the discount stores and sections of supermarkets and large chain stores like K mart and Caldor for closeouts on lipsticks, shampoos, foundations, even whole treatment lines.

You can also purchase house brands that are perfectly excellent substitutes—like Woolworth's brand of talcum powder and baby shampoo—for far less money than the Johnson & Johnson brands. Test. Most baby powders, creams, shampoos are the same. The only real difference may be the cost to you—and that could include the cost of the manufacturer's advertising.

You'll also get the most for your money by simply learning to read labels—not just brand names and slick slogans, not only the instructions, but the *ingredients* listed. Those temporary wrinkle smoothers and hormone-laden creams, the embryonic fluid lotions with odd placental extracts and other exotic names that end in chemical formulas, may be useless and overpriced, and in some cases can even be harmful when applied to the skin. (For instance, any cream containing hormones or steroids is dangerous when used during pregnancy.)

Basically there is no difference in ingredients between high- and low-priced cosmetics and treatment creams. All firms use the same basic contents and bases. In fact, many are made by the same manufacturing plants and only in the packaging state, when the product is aimed toward reaching a specific market, do the real differences begin, and then only in appearance and price.

There is also value to be gained by reading the directions on a product's label. Often, with simple addition and subtraction, you'll find that it pays to spend a bit more on one product that contains richer ingredients. A little, in this case, will go a long way. When the first ingredient you read is water, water is what you're getting. And paying for. Like food packaging the ingredients are listed in order of quantity. Pay attention and you'll be paying less.

Lipstick is lipstick. There is only one way to make it. You may want to pay for a prettier case and a designer label that the manufacturer is paying someone else to design for him. But know that this is basically what you are paying for and not what is inside. Sure, you may want a special shade of pink, but believe me, if you'll look at all the less expensive brands, you'll find that pink. Exactly. Cheaper lipsticks are basically the same as the far more expensive brands, and the color range is extraordinary. Just look in the discount store and count how many variations of red you'll discover. Regardless of cost, lipstick, like all cosmetics, must conform to governmental purity standards. And the competition keeps most cosmetics uniformly good.

In fact, most cosmetic items contain the same emollient bases—all of which can be purchased at a discount store or drugstore at far more reasonable prices. True, some look thicker, but then some are thinner. Some are colored darker, others lighter. Some smell sweeter, others don't have any aroma. Each product may be differently packaged and scented and promoted and priced, but basically all of the products offered in the makeup, skin- and hair-care world contain the same, the very same ingredients. All you may be paying for in additions are more chemical additives, more preservatives, and more advertising that costs more that states more often that the so-called miracle ingredient in the more expensive product is worth it. It isn't.

The Romance in Cosmetics

Why this love affair with cosmetics? The origin and romance and application of cosmetics is as old as vanity itself. For many centuries cosmetics, which is defined in Webster's dictionary as "to finish artistically what nature has left undone" has been synonymous with beauty, romance, illusion, and glamour. Historically the use of cosmetics has been traced to the Atlantians some twenty-three thousand years before Christ. The Chinese later on used artificial methods of enhancing beauty, and this was still some eight hundred years before the Christian era. And the practice of the art was hardly confined to women. Nero, the infamous emperor of Rome, used cosmetics liberally way back in A.D. 54.

And why not. Psychologists today have noted the

positive contribution that cosmetics can give to alleviating depression and helping nervous cases. It is supportive of the emotional health and well-being of most women. In fact, the loss of interest in cosmetics is often the predecessor of a loss of interest in life itself—it seems we want to look good when we feel good, and vice versa. Often if a woman is depressed but she will put on some rouge and lipstick and eye makeup, she'll help to lift her spirits. Try it sometime if you find yourself in a blue mood. It works.

Yes, romance and cosmetics and good health can go together. And so does a positive view of one's self. And so there is really nothing wrong with splurging a bit on that extra-special lipstick color that will look absolutely smashing with that new dress for the party. But there is something smart about learning how to get that extra-special lipstick at half the price.

How to Use This Book

And so, depending upon your age and needs, and your pocketbook, you'll find the less expensive product suggestion and how to use it, within this guide. How to care for your skin, how to make it up, how to do it cheaper and better, is all here for your interest.

The book is divided into sections that cover all of a woman's beauty concerns—from head to toe and in this order. And you will also find special situations addressed separately. So that if you have read and applied how to make up your eyes in Chapter IV but are gaining weight and think you want to see if there's a better way to make up to slim your face, you'll turn to

Chapter VII for the overweight woman. And of course if you don't want to spend any money at all on certain items, turn to Chapter VIII on home remedies and recipes and you'll find lots of kitchen alternatives to the discount-store route.

And so forth. You may read this book from cover to cover, or you might also prefer to read only those chapters that are relevant right now. Read it from back to front or from the middle onward. Whatever your interests are, you'll find the subject carefully and totally covered.

CHAPTER II

Your Hair

The Facts

- The average rate of hair growth is just about a half inch each month.
- Hair actually grows fastest between the ages of sixteen and twenty-four.
- Hair replaces itself approximately a dozen times during the average lifetime.
- Fairy tales or not, a woman's hair has rarely grown longer than three feet.

Expert Tips That Go to Your Head

Doing what comes naturally may be the path to healthy hair as well as skin. Forget about the clichéd rules—like brushing a hundred times a day—and a traditional style. What you need to do to have your hair reflect the best of you, to be your shining glory, is to learn what flatters it most, and then the shortcuts and smart tricks that will help you to do it for yourself. Here, the basic tips I've gleaned from the experts to help you know what's best for your hair:

- It doesn't matter whether you use boar bristles or plastic ones in brushing your hair. What does matter is the strength and the vigor of the brushing, and, no, a hundred strokes a day won't make for shinier hair.

- You can eat your way to healthier hair by having a good balance of proteins, unsaturated fats, fruits, and veggies. You should avoid those foods that contain sugars, and heavy caffeine usage. In fact, if you're prone to flakiness, or any scalp conditions, then more B vitamins and eliminating all coffees, teas, and colas will help. Total, sensible nutrition can make a difference.

- Always towel-dry your hair before blow-drying. Removal of tangles is best with a wide-tooth comb. When blow-drying, be sure to direct the air current at your hair and not at the scalp. Keep your hair dryer in constant motion. Heat concentrated on one spot can be damaging.

- If hair tends to be dry, massage your scalp while drying the hair to stimulate the natural oils. If you have oily hair, then don't use the hottest setting on your blow-dryer, which will only stimulate more oil flow.

- In hot weather sun sparingly. Keep your hair as well covered as possible, even when swimming. Sea water and chlorine from swimming pools can be true villains when it comes to the scalp and hair.

The Art of Illusion

Depending upon your face shape, your hair shape can add or detract. Of course, there is the total you, and even though the rule is to avoid center parts when one has a prominent nose, if you love your hair parted in the center, then keep it that way. However, here are some basic face shapes that are enhanced by the hair that surrounds it. Do you recognize yours?

For a square or heavy/full face: A soft, curvy hairdo that goes around and under the face and falls below the jawline, is a good one for you. You might also try a side part to encourage your hair to fall softly about your eyes and forehead.

For a heart-shaped face: Try a hairstyle that is wider at the bottom than it is at the top. Full, curvy bangs also help. Your hairdo should be smooth on the side and fuller under the jawline, in a sort of "cup shape" at the bottom.

For a round face: Tendrils or softly falling curls that drape about your face at the temples, as well as at the chin, will create the proper effect. You may use a center or side part, depending upon your features.

For a thin or angular face: Try one of those angular geometric cuts. Keep it short, with long bangs that sweep to one side, or, with the back clipped so close that your face will look fuller. You might also angle the hair toward the cheekbones.

Hair Cutting You Can Do at Home

To cut your own bangs neatly and well, all you need is a proper (sharp) pair of scissors, a steady hand, a back hand-mirror setup, and a bit of hair-setting tape that you can purchase at any variety store. This is a youthful look that works well on high foreheads, on pear-shaped or on oval-shaped faces. It sometimes does wonders for long faces, as well. (And it will save you some trips to the hairdresser for an overall cut. All you will have to do is maintain the bangs' neatness in between professional cuttings.)

STEP 1. Comb the area you intend having as bangs forward, then pull the rest of your hair back with a rubber band or some hair clips. Tip: Don't cut the bangs past the natural hairline at each side.

STEP 2. Smooth the bangs down with the palm of your hand, then attach a strip of hair-setting tape about a quarter of an inch above the ends you intend to remove.

STEP 3. Dampen the bangs with a wet sponge. It's far simpler to cut hair in a straight line when the hair is wet.

STEP 4. Start by cutting a small section of the hair right above your nose. Be sure to leave a little extra length, for the hair will seem shorter when it dries.

STEP 5. Now, holding the scissors tightly in your hand, and using the center section where you have just cut as a guide, cut the hair/bangs to the left.

STEP 6. Complete by cutting the remaining bang section to the right. Now, remove the tape and check to be sure it's an even length. Brush to dry.

What About Home Perms?

There are many home permanents you can purchase at the discount store that will create a soft, natural-looking wave and curl and that are quite easy to do on your own, or with a friend to help.

With the ever-rising cost of salon treatments—where permanents can cost anywhere from thirty dollars to more than a hundred dollars, it really pays to invest in a home-permanent kit, which may cost four to seven dollars. Since refills are just three to four dollars, you can see the advantages to your budget. But remember, all the home-perm kits, like Lilt, Toni, Ogilvie, Revlon, and Rave, contain specific directions that should be followed carefully for the best results.

Most home perms contain a nonammonia formula that is gentle to the hair. There are also products like Toni's Lightwaves, which is a one-step, self-timing soft perm that works well on almost all hair types and will last from six to eight weeks. Of course, there are permanents that are more permanent. The diameter of the rod or curler and the amount of the curl wrapped around it will determine the desired wave. Read the description and instructions on the boxes and you'll see kits for gentle, regular, and super waves. There are also products like Milk Wave by Lilt, in this case, a formula with special sensitivity for use on color-treated or damaged hair.

Wash and Wear

If you're looking for a way to deal with fine/limp or just boring/straight hair, then perhaps a soft curl is the answer. You can accomplish a natural-looking wavy style yourself without spending expensive hours at a salon. Most perms will last a good half a year, and that's a lot less than spending your money at the salon. Best of all, a softly permed hairdo is usually a wash-and-wear do, one that is just perfect for the busy woman.

Tip: If you have a curly perm coiffure and need to reactivate it easily all you need do is spritz with water (a plant sprayer works nicely) and the natural wave will bounce right back.

Of course, avoid using any dyes, heavy color treatments or bleaches too soon after perming. You should treat your hair to conditioning before deciding to color it after a permanent. There are many cream rinses and conditioners you can use, like Woolworth's Instant Conditioner Balsam Protein, or Vidal Sassoon Liquid Protein Hair Conditioner, to name just two.

Other product suggestions to condition, clean and care for your hair are Johnson's No More Tangles, a spray-on cream rinse, which is great for all kinds of hair, is easy to use as a styling aid, and imparts shine, body, and manageability. If your hair is badly damaged, then you might need a deep penetrating conditioner. There is Ogilvie's Penetreat, a penetrating reconditioner for the hair, and there is also the Wella Kolestral conditioning cream, which must be left on the hair for a half hour for maximum results. (You can apply this cream after shampooing and, to speed up the penetration, wrap your head in a hot, wet towel after applying the conditioner.)

Home Hair-Care Treatments

A HOT-OIL HAIR-REPAIR SESSION. This one is easy to do at home. Just heat two to four tablespoons (depending upon your hair length) of olive or any vegetable oil, just until the oil gets warm, not hot. Now pour into a small dish. After parting your hair in sections, apply the oil to both your scalp and hairline with a pastry brush or some cheesecloth. Now gently massage your scalp so the oil is distributed throughout your hair. Do this until your scalp feels tingly warm. Finally spread the oil throughout with a wide-tooth comb. Then pile all the hair on top your head, wrap in a piece of plastic, and allow it to seep through your strands for fifteen minutes. Shampoo after and well, at least three times.

QUICKIE MAYONNAISE. Take a cup of your favorite mayonnaise, apply to dry hair, wrap in plastic, massage in, and allow this to stay for a half hour. Shampoo and rinse with a bit of lemon or a one-quarter cup of vinegar added to the final rinse. It will do wonders.

What About Color?

If you've always secretly thought you were really meant to be a blonde instead of a brownette, or a redhead instead of a brunette, or an ash blonde instead of a redhead, but were always afraid to take the plunge, you might try out temporary hair rinses that color gently, or perhaps consider frosting or sun-streaking your hair. Color experts all agree that making drastic changes isn't a good idea. Hair-painting or frosting is usually a better choice for dull shades, for dry hair, and for subtly adding a little lightness at a time.

There are home frosting kits you can purchase, from Clairol and Roux and other manufacturers, which you can use gently. For instance, Clairol makes a product called Quiet Touch Hairpainting, which adds highlights to blond to medium-brown hair. You can also purchase a frosting cap at a beauty-supply store and use this to pull out only certain strands of hair to achieve a highly subtle color.

Where Clairol's Quiet Touch is subtle and works specifically for medium-brown to blond hair, there is also Clairol's Frost & Tip, which works well on just about any hair color. Here, you'll achieve a lighter shade than your own in those strands you choose to streak and highlight. Again, reading the descriptions on the product boxes is always a good idea for gauging whether or not that product is the right one for you. Of course, following the instructions inside is even more important. You really don't want to end up with frizzy, overbleached, or miscolored hair.

As for other conditioners when you need them, Clairol also makes a deep-penetrating one called Condition. In this case, apply after shampooing for at least half an hour, wrapping your head in a towel that is moist/warm. The natural heat of the scalp will help Condition penetrate into the hair shaft.

Precoloring Rules

- Before coloring, make sure your hair is strong and healthy. Dried-out, porous, or weak hair should be preconditioned.
- Follow kit directions to the letter and, if you can, have a friend to help so you don't overdo any of those streaks. Remember, you can always add more on later.
- Always patch-test before coloring, and wait at least twenty-four hours to assure yourself you're not allergic to the product.
- To see how fast your hair takes color, test one strand you're planning to color, bleach or lighten before doing the rest.

Start a Proper Hair-Care Program

Whatever hairstyle you intend to wear, and no matter what color or streaks or perms you might decide to use, what is vital to a good and healthful head of hair is a faithful program of basic hair care. You might want to get your hair analyzed by a professional (which is offered free at major salons across the country). Discuss problems and ask questions and then more questions about your hair. In this manner a professional can suggest a program that you can maintain at home. Take notes if necessary, for the best products and advice won't work for you if you use them improperly.

Remember, don't expect overnight miracles. For damaged hair, for limp, lusterless, and baby-fine hair, the proper conditioning and cut will help, but only with time, tenderness, and constant attention. And don't keep switching products. If you find one or two shampoos or conditioners that work, use them so you can judge what is happening. Don't buy a sale item that just isn't the correct formula for your hair texture. It's best to find the products that work the best and stay with them.

Edward Moore, who is the director of hair coloring for the Vidal Sassoon Salons, has given some wonderful hair treatments that you can do at home. Warns Edward: "Spend some time to be aware of some of the ingredients in the products you use on your hair, body, and skin. People are more aware today of what we put *in* our bodies. Now, let's be aware of what we put *on* our bodies."

Following are some hair treatments you may employ at home. They cost far less than the expensive salon version. All, the courtesy and creation of Edward Moore.

For natural blond hair that is fine and lacks luster and/or body:

Ingredients: 1 pack of neutral henna, which you'll find
at most pharmacies
1 egg
juice of one lemon
brewed warm chamomile tea (make a
strong batch)
4 to 8 oz. unflavored yogurt

Mix all the ingredients in a blender, or large bowl if
you haven't a blender. Make sure that the tea is warm
and apply it that way. After application, cover your
hair with plastic wrap, and sit under a dryer if possible. If not, just wrap a warm towel about the plastic
headdress and leave it on for one hour.

Note: For darker hair tones, the same process can apply. Here, you substitute coffee for the chamomile tea.

Flash: Keep the hennas neutral. If you use a colored
henna powder, consult with a professional first. Even
if you intend to do it yourself, too many mistakes can
be made by applying a wrong color and you'll have to
live with it. An ounce of prevention, here, please.

A fun conditioner for the summer or warm months:

Ingredients: 8 oz. unflavored yogurt
1 teaspoon vitamin E oil
2 tablespoons safflower oil
1 pack of high-quality protein conditioner*

* Vidal Sassoon Protein Pac Treatment is a good one.

Put all these ingredients, after blending well, on hair that is damp. Mush all through the hair and then place a plastic wrap round it, or sit on the beach without the wrap, or out of doors in the sun. Allow to remain for one half hour. After, lightly shampoo to get the oil out, but not so much that you get rid of all that good protein conditioning power.

Here is a light color/conditioner from Edward Moore, for brown hair that has gone brassy after too much sun and exposure:

Ingredients: 1 bottle of nonperoxide color, such as Clairol's Beautiful Browns or Revlon's Young Hair (Choose a shade close to your own)

1 liquid-protein treatment, like Vidal Sassoon Liquid Protein Conditioner

1 pack of protein conditioner (like Sassoon's Protein Pac)

Shampoo your hair gently. Follow up with the liquid-protein treatment for strengthening the hair. Now, rinse, after following the instructions. Apply the color evenly, again carefully using the directions included in the color-treatment package. When color time is completed, follow up with the protein-conditioning pack.

And for Afro hair that has gone dry and brittle, Edward Moore suggests:

Ingredients: 1 application of a liquid henna creme, such as Colora's Henna Creme or any

like product you can find in the discount store or in a beauty-supply shop
(Note: Do not use the powder hennas
for Afro texture hair, as they can dry
it more)
1 pack of protein conditioner

Mix all the ingredients together and apply to freshly
shampooed hair. Make certain you have removed any
oil that was present. Wrap in plastic and leave on the
hair for a half hour. Then rinse. Follow with a good
hair moisturizer like Sassoon's Hair Re-Moisturizing
Creme, and then rinse hair.

Note: Edward recommends that Afro hair be dressed
only with a tiny dab of moisturizer, rather than placing a heavy oil on the hair. Most professional lines of
hair-care products include a hair moisturizer.

Dress Up Your Hair

How about some clever tips to glamorize your hairdo
inexpensively? Coaxing your hair into a holiday mood
or a nighttime look can be cheap chic, if you'll just let
your imagination roam and develop a style that suits
you perfectly. Strive for a sense of balance between
your hair, your makeup, and your clothes; but be sure
you feel one hundred percent comfortable with the total look, so that you're not overdoing too many flowers or ribbons in your hair that take away from your
dress and other accessories. However, handled with

taste, your hair can become the most important beauty
accessory you have. It's all in the magic of experimentation.

Tips for Special Evenings

Try highlighting your hair with a favorite pair of clip-
on earrings, or try two pairs clustered together. To attach them securely in your hair, use an ordinary hairpin. Place it at the end of a very small section of hair.
Now, wrap the ends of the hair around the pin and
wind it tightly into the hair, as you would a roller,
getting as close to the scalp as possible. Bend the ends
of the hairpin in toward the middle, so that the two
ends will meet in the center. This will give you a firm
posting for an earring to clip onto.

You may also braid your hair if it's long enough, or
do a simple chignon in the back, then attach glittery
pins or earrings in the same manner, first making certain the hairpin is secure and will hold your costume
jewelry firmly in your hair.

You might also buy some glittery powder, then carefully paint a few strategic strands with the copper or
gold or silver color and, presto, you'll have a stardust
look in your hair.

And don't forget ribbons—you can save all those
Christmas ribbons and birthday ties, and when you
need a nighttime dynamite look, ribbon some sections
of your hair pertly. Or braid just one or two larger
sections that can frame your face, or atop your head
you can wear a colored ribbon that matches your
dress.

Tips for Holiday Hairdos

First make a thorough investigation of your jewelry box. You'd be surprised at the exciting things you can do with odd pieces of jewelry you may not have worn in years. For instance, braid one section, then slip a beautiful costume ring around and secure it firmly in the hairstyle. Or lace a simple back twist of hair, or a chignon, with a nuggety pearl or rhinestone necklace. And don't forget, you can also use feathers for drama. A few brightly colored feathers can almost serve as a hat, and certainly will do wonders in the back of a chignon.

Then, consider crepe paper, your old friend from the variety store. From chignons to wraps to rolls, you can make a twist of crepe paper into wonderful streamers or fashion them into miniature fans to finish off a holiday hairdo. Also fun items from the supermarket, for those who are daring, are the food colorings you use for icing the cake. Here, you can use a bit of off-green or blue or red or purple color for a temporary and wild accent shade for light-and medium-brown hair. Start with a strand or two, strategically placed.

Veils, standard barrettes tucked into the hair in multiple fashion, stone-studded and plume ornaments you might find in an old box in the attic, bits and pieces of gift box ornaments and ribbons—there are many imaginative and inexpensive ways you can dress up a hairstyle to create a highly personalized fashion for a look that is purely you. Adorning the hair with jewels, even bits of metallic colored paper that you afix to bobby pins and then dress up in your do, will play up the texture and color of your hair, and add just a bit of elegance for those special occasions. Best of all, they're just for that event; and so fresh flowers, glittering combs, or perhaps tumbling curls you ribbon all over—they're all wonderfully temporary, and as inexpensive as your creativity allows you to be.

Brushing Up: Facts and Quick Tips

- No time to wash hair? Cover your hairbrush with a piece of cheesecloth or an old stocking and just brush through. Dirt and oil will be partially absorbed, leaving hair fluffier.
- The greatest number of hairs are lost in March and April, the fewest in July, and the average life of a single hair is a bit over four years.
- Hair is a super place to use perfume. Just spray it on the nape of the neck and around the temples a few moments before going out. Or if you're using ribbons or other hair accessories, try putting a bit of perfume on a small piece of cotton and affixing this to the interior of whatever is holding the hair in place.
- Beer is an excellent setting lotion, as is gelatin and yogurt—a little of each goes a long way, so use sparingly.
- Bangs correct a number of facial flaws—from long faces to high foreheads to bad hairlines to

small eyes to barely-there eyebrows, consider some hair used as a bang. To clean stringy/oily bangs, try cornstarch. A little, sprinkled in your palm and fluffed through the bangs with a brush, will freshen them for the evening.

The Plus-Fifty Factor

If you're over fifty years of age, you'd do well to consider keeping your hair shorter than you may have worn it before; that is, if you have always favored long hair, even to-the-shoulder can be too long when you're over fifty. Most women who want to find the best look for themselves should take the classic approach, and realize, that as we age, less is always more.

Although many women aren't even ready to be really glamorous until after they're reached maturity—from forty years of age up—it's only later that we acquire a special identity and enough self-confidence to keep from following every fad. So what if the trend is to long hair one year—if you're looking your best you'll know that a shoulder-do will heighten any lines and only exaggerate flaws and those down-cast droopy facial shadows. Good form, color that isn't far off from your own natural skin tones that doesn't look unnatural, a healthy texture, and a simple cut that brings out the best of you and your features are the goals you should aim for. Remember that shiny hair, well-shaped and cared for, is a look that is always in style. Hair should be considered as a special fabric, one that can make you look pretty. How much time you will have to spend to maintain a particular look and still to keep your life-style free and easy, are also important factors to consider.

Finally, if you're covering gray, don't try to match your natural hair-color. Instead, use a lighter shade. It will be more flattering to your skin tones and can help you look younger. And if you're going through a blue period, never attempt to drastically change your hair color during a depressed time. You just might not be pleased with the results when your mood lifts. Better to have a fun wig to put on for those real emergency situations—it will save you a lot of grief by experimenting first with a temporary look.

Remember, a very dark or severe shade to the hair will call attention to lines and skin flaws—going a few shades lighter than you were as an adolescent will make any harsh facial lines less obvious. Try temporary rinses first, then see what compliments you get before deciding on any permanent color.

Product Cues

Besides some of the budget-saving products mentioned in this chapter on hair care, here are some others you'll find at your local variety, discount, or supermarket and chain store that can save you money and do a good job.

Tame Conditioning Clean Rinse with Extra Body
Suave Full Body Shampoo for Normal/Dry Hair
Nestle Egyptian Henna Pre-Mixed Finishing Hair Rinse
Nestle Egyptian Henna Conditioning Shampoo

CHAPTER III

Your Precious Skin

Twelve Basic Steps for Healthy Skin

Although we may all be born with perfect, almost poreless skin, as we mature, diet, hormonal changes, pollution, the sun, and such sundry bad habits as smoking and excess drinking can take their toll in large pores, skin eruptions, lines, discoloration, wrinkles, and such. More than likely the area of beauty and good grooming that causes the most confusion among women is that of proper skin care. Unfortunately there are no easy answers to the subject, for skin is very much an individual matter, with certain genetic pluses and minuses having much influence, as well as how we take care of ourselves.

I have asked Dr. Jim Baral, a distinguished New York dermatologist who is an associate in that field at the Mount Sinai Hospital Medical Center in New York, to answer some questions, and to give some good advice on what we can do to take care of our skin the best way we can. Naturally, age, skin type, race, a multitude of factors, must be taken into account. Following are some general tips drawn from information provided by Dr. Baral that should be part of just about every woman's long-range regimen for healthy, supple skin.

1. Moisturize. This is the most important part of your beauty routine. Even the oiliest complexion needs moisture. The drier your skin, the richer moisturizer you'll need. Try to moisturize after cleansing your face in the morning and before applying foundation, then after removing makeup at night, before bedtime. (You may use Cetaphil lotion that you can purchase at almost any drugstore). Or, try any of the basic moisturizing creams, from Pond's Dry Skin Cream to Johnson's Baby Lotion, to any of the Vidal Sassoon skincare products that you'll find in most food and mass retail and discount stores, as well as Cover Girl's or Bonne Bell's moisturizers. There is a wide choice of inexpensive products that do the job.

2. Use an eye cream. The delicate skin under and around your eyes is one that has the fewest natural oil duct glands and so is the thinnest and driest area of facial skin. Here, use a rich and nourishing cream. Some of the products you might try are Johnson's Baby Lotion, or Baby Oil, Pond's Dry Skin Cream, or any good and rich cream that is unscented, rich, and concentrated in strength.

3. Stay out of the sun. Nothing, but nothing, warns Dr. Baral, ages your skin faster than exposure to ultraviolet light. Every minute that you are out in the sun, especially during the harmful 10:00 A.M. to 3:00 P.M. warmer weather hours, the

sun's rays can cause structural damage to your skin. If you must sun, use a good sun blocker, one preferably containing PABA, which is known to help block the sun's harmful rays from the skin. There are many products on the market with the new sun protection factor system that you'll find in the dimestore, everything from Bain De Soleil's Ultra Sun Block Creme, with a sun protection factor of 23.9, to a host of other good products with important sun-blocking power. Read each label carefully.

4. Eat a well-balanced diet. A deficiency in certain vitamins may cause your skin to develop superficial lines and pouches under the eyes, as well as create skin blemishes and rashes. Especially important are foods rich in Vitamins A, C, and E. Don't overdo the A and E; they may be toxic in cumulative doses. Vegetables and fruits are good sources, and of course, stay away from deep-fried foods, sugars, and white starch products.

5. Drink plenty of water. This will keep your skin from drying out and help rid it of impurities.

6. Stop smoking. Studies show that women who smoke develop lines, like those pout lines about the lips, much faster than women who don't. Your skin will also develop a yellow cast if you smoke a lot.

7. Use a mild abrasive on your skin. Since men shave almost daily, and some men twice daily, often this mild abrasion of shaver against the skin keeps their complexions appearing younger by removing dead skin cells. You can achieve the same effect by using a bit of cornmeal or oatmeal

mixed in water as your own homemade beauty grains. Cleanse your face with this mixture weekly. Avoid the delicate area around your eyes. You should also get into the habit of using a rough washcloth and soap for your face if it is oily, followed by a mild astringent like witch hazel, adds the doctor.

8. Exercise. Jog, play tennis, learn how to play racquetball, golf, swim; whatever keeps your body moving will help your skin have better circulation, which is the key to a good complexion.

9. Exercise your facial muscles. Pursing your lips as if you're ready to kiss is good, as is opening your mouth as wide as you can. A few simple exercises like these can help keep your skin supple. (We are going to give you a couple of good facial exercises to practice, later on in this chapter.)

10. Purchase a small humidifier for your home if you live in a dry climate, or if you live in an area where you have heated rooms in the colder months. Dry air causes the skin to dehydrate and that causes lines to develop. A good humidifier can keep the hair moist as well as protect your skin.

11. Get enough sleep. Burning the candle at both ends will make you look old before your time. Your eyes and your skin are the first indicators of poor sleeping habits. Regular sleep patterns, rather than sleeping ten hours one day to make up for no sleep the prior, is best for your complexion and your general health.

12. Try sleeping on your back. When you sleep with your face pressed to the pillow it only in-

creases the pressure upon it and the opportunity of developing puffiness, lines, and wrinkles. It takes time to develop a comfortable sleep if you're not used to sleeping with two or three pillows raised under your head, face up, but it's well worth the practice.

Remember, says Dr. Jim Baral, the skin deserves the best possible care you can lavish on it, and an ounce of prevention is worth a pound of products and cure.

Skin Profiles

It is important to classify your skin type with accuracy, for it is worthless to purchase a good moisturizer to use all over if in fact all over is not where you need it. Most women don't have clear-cut types of skin—but rather combination skin with oily areas and drier patches. Only as we grow older do we usually acquire drier skin. This is caused by the slowing down of the sebaceous glands and their oil output, as well as to a general decrease in collagen, those fiberous structures within the skin that keep it elastic, and finally, to the evaporation of too much water within the skin's cells. Following are some basic skin profiles for you to read and compare and see where you fit in.

DRY SKIN: Your face is dry in the middle portion (nose, forehead) as well as on the sides. It often feels tight and taut and can easily get rough and parched. You may notice fine wrinkling around your eyes, as well as the corners of your mouth. And your face chaps in the winter and is prone to sunburn in the sun. Sometimes the texture of your face looks dull or coarse, and it can get flaky and feel uncomfortable periodically.

ULTRA-DRY OR DEHYDRATED SKIN: You have all of the characteristics of the dry-skin profile, but you also have skin that is ready to or already shows signs of wrinkling, and if you use regular soap and water to cleanse it, your face feels almost like a desert. You tend to have problems with low-humidity areas, with overheated rooms, with sun. You may also suffer from skin conditions like eczema or dandruff on the scalp. Your skin is so ultrasensitive that most makeups must be oil-based and hypo-allergenic and even then you find your eye shadow caking in the creases and your face looking like an overly made-up doll. You must be careful with makeup application and always apply a good moisturizer as a base.

NORMAL TO DRY SKIN: The T-zone portion of your face (the central portion which includes nose and forehead) is somewhat oily, including the chin, while the major portion is slightly dry. Your nose area may be prone to blackheads, clogged pores and you may have some blemishes on the chin, while the upper lip area, the area around your eyes and your neck tend to be dry.

NORMAL SKIN: You have a general all-over consistency to the texture and feel of your skin, which is neither too oily or too dry. It tends to be fine-textured with few enlarged pores and is smooth to the touch. It often has a fine glow and the surface appears like "peaches and cream." You really have no major problems with blemishes, no oily film, and your pores are rarely clogged or enlarged. Your makeup goes on easily and stays. Your skin is healthy and glowing, has good elasticity, which ensures suppleness, and functions in a natural manner. You're a lucky lady.

NORMAL TO OILY SKIN: Your face is subject to a light shine in the T-zone, while the sides can range from normal to even dry. You tend to have a buildup of blackheads or pimples on the forehead and around the nose, and you may have enlarged pores. These enlarged pores can turn into problem areas, while your neck and upper lip area can remain dry and require a different kind of care, as will the area around your delicate eyes.

OILY SKIN: Your skin just has too much of a good thing: oil. The forehead, nose, chin, cheeks, and below the cheekbone area are almost constantly oily. You also have enlarged pores due to dilation from too much oil. You may have either occasional or frequent skin eruptions, from blackheads to plugged whiteheads to blemishes. You are also prone to a superfluous hair growth on the upper lip and chin as you age. Your skin can become sluggish, losing elasticity as the pores fail to function properly. In extreme cases you develop adult acne, or pustules and boils that can result in lesions and scars as they eventually become infected and fester before they heal.

How to Typecast Your Skin

After reading these descriptions, if you're still not certain of the category that best describes your skin, you can try two simple tests. First, use regular soap and water, and cleanse your face well, really well. Follow by rinsing at least a dozen times with lukewarm water. Wipe dry and then wait at least a half hour before examining it to see if there are areas that seem to be less dry than others. How? Take a simple piece of paper, either purchase some of those cigarette papers for people who roll their own, or try to find a good-quality, thin tissue paper. Using either slip of paper, gently press against the various areas on your face checking after each application of paper to see if any oil has collected. This should help you determine if your T-zone is oilier than the rest of your face, if all of your face is oily, and so on. Test until you're certain that the skin has thrown off all the oil beneath the surface. In some cases, where the skin is very oily, within fifteen minutes of soap and water washing, you'll collect oil on the paper. The mild to maximum amount of oiliness of your skin will be determined by just how much oily film you can collect and in how much time, on each specific area of your face.

Rating the Products, from Creams to Soaps

Many cosmetic manufacturers claim that their creams contain the magic ingredients that will erase wrinkles, soften the skin, and make a woman look like a movie star, if only she will use it faithfully. Of course, when the cream costs seventy-five dollars for a precious ounce, one would think that there really was a magic ingredient in the cream.

Nonsense! There are no magic ingredients, no panacea, no special formula gel, potion, lotion, or cream that can make you young again, or keep you young, or make you more beautiful than you are, or that works better than another. Sure, some creams work more effectively upon one type of skin than another. This is an individual matter, where some skin types need richer ingredients, while others need a milder formula. But whether a cream costs twenty dollars or two dollars, the end result is the same; in fact, in many cases, the cheaper, the better, because there is less likely to be any harsh preservatives and potentially harmful hormones in them.

And so you can go to the dime or discount or chain store and purchase Pond's Creamy Facial Cleanser, Noxzema Raintree Concentrated Moisture Maker for Extra Dry Skin, Johnson's Baby Oil, or a house brand baby oil, and, even a big jar of Vaseline Pure Petroleum Jelly. You will get the same good effects as you will from (the double, triple, and ten times the price) creams with the designer label and expensive packaging that promise you eternal allure in the ads. Remember, often you're paying for the expensive labels, packages, and advertising that promotes these deluxe products—there is no difference in what they can do for *you*.

As for soaps and shampoos, the same general rules apply. For instance, when it comes to soaps, almost all do an equally good job of cleansing. What you require is mildness, and this doesn't necessarily mean the most expensive nor the soap that is advertised as the mildest. And if you have sensitive or dry skin, mild does matter. Certain soaps that have been touted as being the mildest, like Ivory and Neutrogena, were recently tested and found lacking. In order of mildness, there is Dove, the mildest, then Aveenobar, Dial, and Alpha Keri.

Shampoos are liquid soaps. Most list extravagant claims for their ingredients, including repairing damaged hair. No one has proved they can do this, and since hair is dead tissue, there is little scientific rationale in repairing what is already dead, nor can they coat the hair, since the nature of a shampoo is to remove, not deposit material. A basic shampoo, followed by a homemade conditioning treatment, with either mayonnaise or egg or yogurt or oil, can give your hair some body and protection. You can also purchase medicated shampoos to help with dandruff or other scalp disorders. These are effective, but that is because they contain chemical ingredients specifically included to arrest the problems.

Facial Muscle Exercises

How to keep the muscles of your face and neck in a healthy condition and even improve muscle tone? The same way you keep your body in top shape—by steady, sensible movements done on a daily basis. Here are two that will help two sensitive areas—one for the upper lip, the other for the chin and neck. Practiced each, for just five minutes, once a day, can help firm those muscles under the chin as well as keep your nasal-labial lines (from nose to mouth) and upper lip area, smoother and firmer.

OPEN AND CLOSE NECK FIRMER. Raise eyebrows high. Now stretch your neck up and hold head straight up. Open your mouth and at the same time stretch your neck forward as far as you can go. Now, close your mouth. Repeat the same sequence, first tilting head back, now stretching the neck up, then opening the mouth while your eyebrows are raised high, again moving your neck forward, just like an ostrich. Repeat as many as twenty times or for about five minutes, slowly and well.

PUCKER-UP MOUTH AND LIP FIRMER. This one is simple. Look straight in a mirror, head straight, standing up. Now, pucker up just like you're going to kiss your absolutely favorite man. Hold this for a count of ten. Release. Repeat at least twenty times.

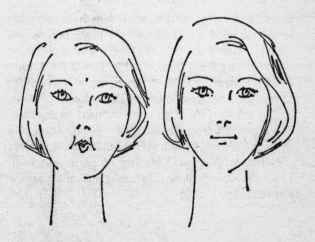

The Importance of Clean Skin

Whether or not you wear makeup, you must keep your skin clean. A fine complexion is quite dependent upon proper cleansing. Between pollution, the fatty and heavy foods we eat, and our natural problems—from oily skin to too dry skin, keeping the skin squeaky clean will serve as a protective measure, besides giving you a fresh and feminine appearance. Removal of makeup is vital, of course. Never, but never, go to sleep with remnants of pore-clogging foundation nor your eye and cheek makeup—it will be imbedded in the skin by morning, never mind on your sheets. Whether you choose a cleansing lotion, cream, or soap, find one that will remove the day's accumulation of grime, dirt, and whatever makeup you have applied.

MORNING CLEANSING PROGRAM. If you have dry skin and have cleansed your face well the night before, you may use a cotton ball saturated with a gentle cleansing lotion, anything from Bonne Bell's Ten-O-Six Lotion to Pond's Creamy Facial Cleanser, or if you prefer soap, you can use Aveenobar or Dove Soap, followed by a good moisturizer. If you have normal to dry skin, the same general instructions apply. If you have oily or normal to oily skin, then you should wash well with soap, follow with a good rinsing of plain water, finally, a mild astringent or skin freshener before applying any makeup.

EVENING CLEANSING PROGRAM. Whether or not you have the type of skin that needs a soap-and-water cleansing, it is suggested that your makeup be removed first with a gentle cleansing cream, oil, or lotion. You might prefer Pond's Cold Cream or Noxzema or any one of a dozen reasonably priced creams and lotions that do a gentle but good job of removing the makeup. It is how you remove the makeup and follow up that is important here.

First, remove the cream or lotion you have smoothed on your face using the tips of your fingers and gently, with damp cotton balls, wiping upward, with long, fluid strokes. Then, if you want to follow with a soap-and-water wash, do so. After, apply a gentle toning lotion to assure that every trace of dirt and makeup has truly disappeared. Here you can choose any nonalcoholic astringent, or try some witch hazel, grandma's own astringent. Why so many steps? Because you'll often find traces of rouge, or a bit of mascara left, even after you've used those commercial eye makeup remover pads or a bit of oil on a tissue—the astringent is the final and best way to remove the stubborn traces often left with the residue of oil.

After cleansing well, apply moisturizer to those dry areas of your skin, and a special eye cream to the sensitive area about your eyes.

Some other products you can consider are Nivea Skin Oil and Nivea Creme, Johnson's Baby Soap and Baby Cream, and Cover Girl moisturizers and creams.

Those Tiny Bumps and How to Get Rid of Them

They're more than likely whiteheads, those tiny, whitish bumps under the skin. Most often they are found in oily skin areas. Why? Waxy plugs remain trapped beneath the surface, rather than coming out through the pore openings. To prevent this from happening, or to properly clean out those that have already lodged there, you might use cleansing grains or granules at least once weekly. A cheap home recipe that works: Make up your own cleanser by mixing a half cup of steel-cut oatmeal with enough tepid water to make a workable paste; if you have highly sensitive skin, then use milk instead of water; it soothes.

If those tiny bumps are deeply imbedded, and they still don't come out, never, but never squeeze. Consult a good dermatologist instead, who will clean them for you and recommend the proper aftercare program.

The Sun and Your Skin

According to leading dermatologists like Dr. Jim Baral, it is the sun that is the major cause of skin wrinkling. The skin never forgets an insult. And overexposure to its harmful ultraviolet rays is indeed an insult of the highest order. Actually, says Dr. Baral, it is a cumulative process that disrupts the connective tissue that supports the skin. Because this damage isn't obvious to the human eye until years later, women still fail to understand how much real damage they're doing to their skin.

The degree to which your skin can tolerate sun is genetically predetermined. Fair-skinned women, particularly those of Celtic background, naturally have less pigment and the skin can't form what is called the melanin to protect itself as easily as someone with black or olive skin. That is why the black woman's skin is protected to a greater degree from the sun and from the more visible signs of aging.

How then can you best protect your skin from the elements? By using a good sun-block product, anything that contains PABA, and one preferably with a sun factor of 15 or higher, will offer the best protection. But one must be sensible too. Besides reading labels, you must know that the rays are filtered through the atmosphere during the summer months or in instances when the ozone layer is thinner. You should avoid the period from ten in the morning until four in the afternoon on those hot dog days; also be aware that reflections from both snow, as well as sand, can have quite the same impact as direct light.

There are many excellent sun-screening products in a discount store that do the job well. Read your labels, find the type that works best for you, and then use it generously and often and whenever your delicate skin is exposed to the sun.

Do-It-Yourself Facial Mask Treatments

Strawberry and Yogurt Facial Mask
Take 2 tablespoons plain yogurt, add 2 tablespoons
fresh strawberry juice, and stir by hand until smooth.
Then, add one egg white and beat to a stiffer consistency. Apply to face and neck, avoiding eye area. Try
cucumber slices or cooled used-tea bags on the eyes,
then lie back, think beautiful thoughts, take ten to
twenty minutes out of your busy day, and relax. After,
rinse off with water that has a half a lemon squeezed
in, which will give you sparkle and return the acid
mantle balance to your skin.

Special Formula Yeast Mask for Dry Skin
This mask can help replenish dried-out skin and help
add topical nourishment to your face. If you have prematurely aging skin, dry skin, or hypersensitive skin,
use this mask weekly for maximum benefit.

> 1 tablespoon plain yogurt
> 1 tablespoon brewer's yeast (purchase in health-
>   food store)
> The contents of one capsule each of Vitamins
>   A, D, and E (400 units)
> 1 egg yolk

Mix these ingredients well. Gently pat on face and
neck area avoiding only the delicate areas around eyes
and lips. Allow to remain on at least fifteen minutes,

or until the mask is completely dry. Gently wash off with mineral water at room temperature. (You might purchase some mineral water and put it in a plant spray bottle to use for spraying your face after makeup, and as a rinse for masks like this.)

Now, pierce another vitamin E capsule (100 units) and apply with your fingertips to the delicate skin areas of the eyes and nasal-labial lines (that run from nose to mouth). Your skin will respond to this treatment if you use it faithfully at least once weekly. By the way, the vitamin E capsule makes a super eye treatment used nightly in the same manner.

Pineapple Cleansing Mask Treatment
This refreshing mask is good for all skin types. The natural enzymes in the pineapple help remove the dead surface cells and clarify the complexion. First, cut up a large slice of pineapple that has been both peeled and cored and whip it to pulp consistency in the blender, or by mashing it finely with a fork. Drain off any excess juice before applying to your face. By the way, you can substitute a half an avocado or a half of papaya fruit. Used in the blender and applied fresh to the face, you'll also get a cleansing, refreshing result. Allow this mask to remain on at least twenty minutes. Remain in a reclining position, since it tends to crumble and can get messy. Rinse off with a half solution of mineral water and half a squeezed and strained lemon, and you'll have a squeaky clean face.

Your Emotions Affect Your Skin

You bet they do. That's why rashes, hives, all sorts of breakouts, can be a symptom of a fear, a worry, a problem that you're not dealing with and that is erupting on the skin. For not all skin problems are physical; some indeed are psychosomatic. These are the ones dermatologists find the most difficult to cure. Before the eruption will disappear, the doctor has to find out how to eliminate the emotional disturbance. You can help. Do you find blemishes popping out after an argument, or after eating junk foods because you were bored or upset or angry? Do you then get an awful case of the hives? Write down in a daily journal the cause and possible effects of each food and pill you take in, as well as each skin problem it might be causing. You can take this journal to a dermatologist or allergy specialist who will find it easier to help you help yourself.

Blushing, although not an ailment, is one common illustration of how the emotions, in this case awkwardness, self-consciousness, and embarrassment can affect the skin. Sweating of the palms before a school test or an important meeting is another symptom. This is often due to anxiety. Many doctors maintain that stress, body chemical change, or vulnerability to some particular germ may cause one part of the body, in this case, the largest organ of all, the skin, to break down. It is believed that upset emotions can trigger or aggravate a wide variety of skin problems, so if you're suffering from a severe case of adult acne, or an allergic reaction that results in hives, eczema, or psoriasis, you would do well to become aware of what is getting to you, literally, under your skin.

How Does a Moisturizer Work?

As we've already said, no matter what type of skin you have, it needs moisture. That's why it's suggested that you learn as well as you can the exact skin type you have, and at the least, if you have very oily skin, use a moisturizer in those areas that are dry or drier.

A moisturizer is designed to help the skin retain a normal amount of water. It can have both an internal and external effect. Externally, it forms a coating on the skin surface to prevent a loss of moisture through evaporation. Internally it helps to activate the underlayers to make better use of body moisture, and may help also to plump out the tissues, to fill those tiny surface lines. A good method of getting the most out of any moisturizer is to seal it with a spray of water.

You'll find a wealth of moisturizers at the discount stores, everything from Bonne Bell to Nivea to Raintree to Max Factor to Natural Wonder to Woolworth's and Lamston's and Caldor's own brands.

The Most Essential Skin Beauty Product

Is water. Drink a great deal of it each day, both tap and mineral and herbal teas too. Water keeps your system clean, aids digestion, and elimination and acts as an internal moisturizer for your skin. You can get into the good habit of squeezing half a lemon into a cup of boiled water each morning and drinking this fifteen minutes before breakfast. It's a good start for the day and helps with elimination. And if your digestive system isn't tops, try a tablespoon or two of bran flakes (you can purchase a cheap bag of bran at the health-food store; refrigerate to keep fresh) each morning, either mixed in yogurt or in your morning cereal or drink.

You might carry a small atomizer of water with you and spray your face with a fine mist three or four times a day. Try cleaning out an old cologne atomizer and filling this with mineral water. The central heating and air conditioning systems in our offices and homes are very drying on the skin, as well as on the nasal and throat passages. Spraying your face gently through the day will give you a superportable humidifier that works. Remember, moisturizing from within, by drinking at least eight glasses of water each day, and from without by spraying with some water, are some of the best ways to keep your skin young and fresh looking.

Handle with Care

Yes, the cardinal rule is to keep the skin clean. Cleaning your face in the morning and the evening is vital. Also important is how you touch your face and the method in which you apply creams and makeup. Here are some special tips:

- When cleaning or applying lotions or cream around the eye area, hold the skin at the outside corner of the eye, and with gentle strokes, wipe inward toward the bridge of the nose. Do this both above and below the eye socket.

- When you put on or remove lotions or creams, never, but never, rub your skin back and forth. Rather, apply the creams in long, fluid strokes, with fingers gentle as feathers, moving upward against the force of gravity. The slightest touch is all you need and a bit of patience and time to do the job right and lovingly.

- Never put heavy creams around your eyes at night. A heavy overly rich cream suffocates the skin and can even make your lids swell by morning. Instead, choose a very light moisturizer, one that is quickly absorbed into the skin.

On Adult Acne

Although young males may have more severe cases of acne, the condition is likely to subside as the adolescent period passes. But with the female, the skin, which matures more slowly, can reduce acne at a slower rate and leave damage, like pits and scars, behind. These can be treated by a dermatologist later. But what about those other cases, where either because of hormonal causes, or those unknown and stressful situations, one suffers from adult acne? Just exactly—what is acne?

Acne, according to Dr. Baral, starts in a sebaceous follicle—a tiny pocketlike skin pore that produces sebum, a natural fatty secretion that keeps skin supple but at the same time can make it far too oily. Or it might begin in a pilosebaceous follicle, one of the glands that boasts a tiny, frail hair.

The follicle becomes plugged with sebum mixed with fine skin debris forming a tough, waxy plug that is called a comedo. When the tip of the plug forces its way through the pore opening, the top darkens, and a blackhead is the result. The following stages of acne include inflammation and even rupture of the gland, causing swelling and redness and leading to tiny wells of pus, bacterial infection, and an unsightly complexion.

It's wise to have medical treatment for acne at any age, advises the doctor. You may be able to shorten the attack and ward off scarring. There are many topical ointments and new techniques that, although they may not yet offer a magic cure to this skin disease, will help clear up some of the problem.

If you suffer from severe oily skin and breakouts, it would be wise to consult with a doctor, and to avoid using harsh makeup at this time. A bit of moisturizer where your skin is still dry, a good oil-reduction astringent, and some of the medicated soaps and creams that are made by Noxzema and Bonne Bell can offer some temporary relief. There are also excellent colored astringents you may use as a foundation, or you can try making your own by mixing a bit of face powder in a color that matches your skin tone into some witch hazel lotion and then mixing well, shaking the bottle lots, and then applying.

Your Basic Face Shape

Now that I've covered the subject of overall skin care, we're ready to move on to the art of making up to show off your prettiest points. But one last step remains: Take a good long look at yourself—what shape is your *face* in?

There are actually as many individual shapes as there are snowflakes. However, we do see some common shapes to the face, from basically oval to basically square to basically diamond shape to basically pear-shaped. Since we are going to learn all we can about how to use makeup properly and try out tricks in application, we should start first by trying to determine our basic shape. Following are some sketches of the six shapes that are most seen. Study them. Look at each. Which is most like your own?

WHICH FACIAL TYPE BEST MATCHES YOUR FACE SHAPE?

- Round? This is a short, broad face that tends to have full cheeks. You might also be overweight and have a full under-chin.
- Square? Then your face is almost equally distant between your forehead and your jawline. The sides of your face are probably angular.
- Heart-Shaped? Then you have a wide forehead with full cheeks, a narrow jawline, and more than likely high cheekbones.
- Diamond-Shaped? Here, your cheekbones are high and wide but your chin is pointed, and

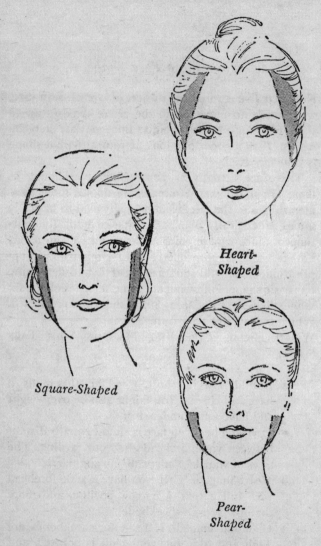

**Heart-
Shaped**

Square-Shaped

**Pear-
Shaped**

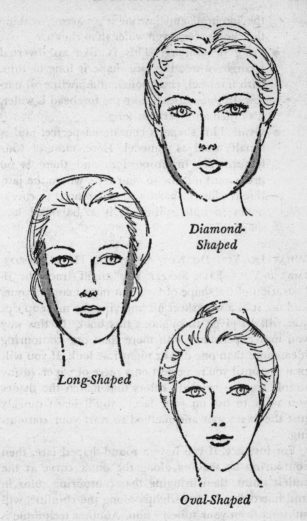

Diamond-
Shaped

Long-Shaped

Oval-Shaped

the forehead and jawline are narrow, making
the cheeks seem even wider than they are.

- Long or Oblong? This is like an inverted
  triangle, where the face shape is long or thin,
  with forehead, cheekbones, and jawline all narrow. In some cases, where the forehead is wider,
  it's called an inverted triangle.
- Oval? This shape is considered perfect and is
  usually used as a model. Here, most of your
  features are in proportion, and there is no
  prominent outline to your face, where the jawline is wider or narrower, or forehead or cheekbones so outstanding. It is a balanced face
  shape.

WHAT DO YOU DO NOW THAT YOU HAVE APPROX-
IMATED YOUR FACE SHAPE? You might trace the illustration of the shape of face that most matches yours
and use it as a worksheet for applying the makeup tips
you will be given throughout this book. In this way
you may experiment with more than one contouring
idea, more than one day or nighttime look. If you will
practice until you're perfect on a piece of paper (using
simple crayons or chalk colors that match the shades
you want to use on your face), you'll learn quickly
just the exact spot and method to start your contouring.

For instance, if you have a round-shaped face, then
contouring by shading along the outer curve at the
fullest point, then bringing that contouring color in
and narrowing it very slightly along the chinline, will
subtract from your fullest point. Another technique is
to begin the contouring at the center of the cheeks and
moving the contour color out to the top of the ears.

Naturally, when you use real contouring color, perhaps a deep rose or taupe shade on your cheeks, you'll have to blend well, and apply a gentle amount of powder to soften the contouring line. Whatever you use of what you will learn, remember that one of the most important rules in contouring is to soften and to blend—never to allow harsh, definite lines that obviously show where your makeup begins or ends.

In the following chapters on makeup you will be shown examples of contouring for each of the face shapes given here. That is why it is suggested that you copy the shape that best matches yours—so you can play around as much as you like and still have the original for tracing when you need it.

CHAPTER IV

Making Up

FOUNDATION/BASE/POWDERS

The illusion of makeup begins with foundation. Just as a building needs a firm supportive base, so your makeup needs the correct shades and type of base to support and hold the rest of the rouge, eye makeup, and lipstick. Choosing exactly what's right for your individual skin is an important factor here. There are dozens of types of foundations and powders. You'll find creamy bases, oil- and water-base foundations, colored astringents for problem skin, skin pastes and liquid concealers, translucent or transparent face powders, cake makeup and pressed powders—a wealth of products from which to choose, and all available in the dime and discount and chain stores. Each can camouflage poor skin, be the canvas for the rest of your makeup application.

Your first decision will be to choose between a water- or oil-based foundation. By now you should have determined whether you skin is basically dry or oily (see Chapter III, page 50, for the skin-type test) . If you have oily skin, then consider using a colored astringent or a water-base makeup made specifically to counteract oily skin. Products like Cover Girl Oil-Control Make-Up with a special water-base formula usually won't go orangey and will give oil-controlled coverage that lasts all day. For dry skin try a creamy foundation by Maybelline or Natural Wonder. If you have aging skin, then a cream foundation will give more coverage and a nicer finish. Following is a list of some of the foundation products you'll find in your dime and chain discount stores:

Foundations
Bonne Bell Medicated Make-Up with Sun Screen
Maxi Unshine Oil-Free Make-Up
Cover Girl Oil Control Make-Up
Natural Wonder Fresh-All-Day Oil-Blotting Makeup
Glowing Finish All-in-One Makeup
Maybelline Oil-Control Make-Up
Colláge Moisture Base Make-Up
Maxi Moist Make-Up
Cover Girl Liquid Make-Up
Posner Liquid Make-Up
Ultra Sheen Liquid Make-Up
Maybelline Moisture Whip Make-Up
Chap Stick Make-Up

You can see from the list above how many types of foundations you'll find. Now, how to use and choose the best one for you.

Face Facts

Good makeup should neutralize yet awaken the color of your skin, make your face glow and look more alive. In most cases choosing a color of foundation that is closest to your natural skin tone is best. In this manner, by blending down to the jawline and neckline you will achieve an all-over natural look. However, if you have a sallow or olive complexion, choose a foundation with more pink color in it. Similarly, if you have a ruddy, pink-splotched skin tone, then choose a foundation with more yellow or beige in it. The truly light and pale skin will benefit from an ivory tone, but do avoid that plaster of Paris look that comes from choosing a foundation that is far lighter than your skin. Remember, what you want to achieve is a natural look. Look at the list given above for only a few of your choices of those manufacturers of inexpensive foundations.

Try Before You Buy

It is best for you to sample makeup to avoid costly mistakes. Most manufacturers offer sample sizes and/ or have counter displays with samples available. Try them. Apply to a small area on one side of a clean face and then study it. If you see an obvious patch of color, one that doesn't match the rest of you, you know this won't do. Keep on trying with simple dabs until you

find one makeup foundation that is the closest to your
own skin tone and will be the least visible with all day
and night wear.

How to Apply Foundation

After you have chosen the correct type and shade for
your skin, you need to know the basics of how to apply foundation in order for it to sit well on your face.
Of course, there should be no visible demarcation
edges. If you have dry skin, you'll want to start with
an all-over moisturizer before applying foundation. Or
apply a bit of baby oil to those really dry areas,
around the nose or eyes. And if you have problem
areas of blemishes, you might want to use a medicated
astringent or paste first to cover or protect these. As
for contouring your face, contour powder is applied
after the foundation. First, learn to apply foundation
well, then find out all the how-tos of contouring in
the very next section.

First, dot the cream or liquid foundation of your
choice on your chin, nose, forehead, and cheek area.
Use the pads of your fingers (so you won't scratch
your face with your nails). Apply the foundation sys-
tematically. Fingertips are really the best method, because the skin warms up naturally, making the
makeup blend better on your face. Gently, using upward motions, cover your entire face, except for the
delicate eye and eyelid areas.

You might begin at the chin, working the foundation well over the jawline, and then continue up to the
curve of your cheeks. Make sure that you cover the

sides of your face, by the hairline and over the temple and forehead, as well as the sides of the nose and the upper-lip area. Use a magnifying mirror and when possible apply all makeup in daylight; perhaps by a window, to assure that you're covering the entire area smoothly and all over.

Be sure to pay special attention to those areas at the side of your nose, below your earlobes, and to the edge of your jawline, blending the foundation especially well here. There is nothing that looks worse than a wonderful makeup application with a few dark patches of extra heavy foundation that haven't been blended well, or a few empty areas where the foundation missed being applied at all. Study yourself after in the mirror and make sure you have done a smooth, translucent job.

Follow this up with a good spritz with a prepared bottle (you can always use a plant sprayer or even an ironing spray bottle) of lukewarm water. Gently applied, a light spray will add just a bit of moisture to your foundation and help set it.

Consider that your foundation has been perfectly applied when it has covered the entire area, including any flaws or blemishes, and is almost invisible, giving your face a harmony of tone. As in all good making up, less is more, and so it would be better to use a fine, translucent makeup base that gently covers, than a heavy, thick swath of foundation that does little more than suffocate the pores beneath and give you an overly made-up look.

Special Tips

1. If your foundation base changes color to orange or pink after it has been on the skin awhile, it really contains too much color for your particular skin tone and type. Better to match your skin with a foundation that has a tannish tone—one that is either light beige or in a taupe shade will usually diminish any orange or pinkish overcasts.

2. If your foundation becomes shiny or wears off too quickly, then more than likely you are using too much moisture cream before applying the foundation, or your skin is oilier than you think and you need to find a water-base oil-control makeup that is more compatible.

3. If your foundation lodges in creases or accents any wrinkles or lines, then it is obviously too drying or too thick for your type of skin. Better to use no foundation at all than to use one that accentuates the negative. Or if you can't find a good oily base that illuminates your skin, try using the foundation lightly and only in those spots that need doing, in a spot application rather than all over.

4. If the foundation doesn't go on evenly, then again, like the tip for point #3, you may need to upgrade your makeup foundation for oily quality, as well as stepping up your own moisturizing program. Most dry skins don't take makeup foundation evenly, unless you properly primp it beforehand with a good moisturizing lotion.

Tinted Under-Makeup Moisturizers

There are special skin pastes and toners available that
do well on dry skins and in spotty dry-skin areas. You
can find liquid, cream, and gel bases that you can use
in addition to your regular moisturizer, depending
upon your particular skin type. Bonne Bell, Maybelline, and, Max Factor all make products that can serve
as underbases. Also there are theatrical types of colored moisturizers that you can adapt to color-correct
your skin if you have a really odd color problem. For
instance, if you have a downright florid complexion—
many ruddy pink or red blush spots, then you might
apply a light green-colored moisturizer to tone down
the reddish look. Similarly, yellow- or sallow-looking
skin does well with a blue or lavender shade of moisturizer. If you can't find these private-label brand
special-colored moisturizers, try using a bit of the
creamy eye shadows you're using for your eyelids in a
fingertip dab application. For instance, a Maybelline
cream eye shadow in aqua tones can be used to diminish the yellow-looking skin tones, and you can use a
FlameGlo light-green eye cream shadow for taking the
reddish tones down a bit.

Tricks of the Trade

Here, some more tips on foundations by international makeup artist Ted Nadel:

- For oily skins an astringent-based foundation is great. However, watch out that they don't contain too much alcohol, which dries the skin temporarily, but then actually stimulates the oil glands. Use witch hazel or low-alcohol-based colored astringents or makeup products, and learn to read the ingredients posted on each label. And always buff with a cotton ball or a clean complexion brush to smooth out any pasty look.
- In the evening, foundation can be highlighted by pearlized translucent powders or blushers.
- During the day, makeup should look fresh and not overdone or contoured. Badly contoured faces look dirty in the daylight.
- If you want to copy a model or actress you see in a magazine, and adapt some of her makeup looks, then turn the beauty shot upside down and you'll find it easier to copy. The blending, contouring and overall shapes become much clearer in this manner.
- Black women should never try to overlighten their complexions. If anything, warm it up with golds, coppers, and bronzes. Avoid any foundation that is lighter than your skin, as it will look pasty.

Powders and How to Use Them

Finishing off the makeup foundation and the rest of
the face is always done best with a dusting of face powder. A transparent, no-color powder is always usable,
although some skin tones do better with a colored
powder that adds the proper beige or pink cast. Here
again, you should try out a number of brands and
tints to see which works best for you. Of course, you
can always use talcum powder or Johnson's Baby Powder or a house brand baby powder can work just as
well on the face. Here is a brief list of some of the
face-powder types and brands you'll find at the stores:

Powders
Bonne Bell Translucent Face Powder
Cover Girl Oil Control Powder
Cover Girl Moisture Encapsulated Powder
Posner Pressed Powder
Posner Blush Powder
Ultra Sheen Pressed Powder
Constance Carroll Powder
Angel Face Powder
Lady Esther Face Powder
Revlon Oil Blotting Powder
Maybelline Moisture Whip Powder

A fresh cotton ball that is dipped into the powder of
your choice, with the excess shaken off, is your best
technique for light dusting. Or get one of those make-

up brushes from Mod or the artist's type in real camel
or sable hair; about two inches wide. Use the brush to
dust the powder gently all over. Don't ever rub or
fluff powder on or it will collect in those dry, fine
line places and hold thickly there. All you want to
achieve with the face powder is take off some of the
shine and hold the foundation and makeup in place.

Shiny surfaces are sometimes good for your particular look, since they tend to appear larger, while flat,
matte finishes will look smaller. And so if you have a
large nose, you'll want to powder it more, while a
small chin or forehead will probably be more appealing if you don't powder those areas at all.

Compressed powders like Pond's and Cover Girl are
perfect for touch-ups and for carrying in your handbag for later use. However, you're best off keeping a
cotton ball in the compact and using a new one daily.
Powder puffs collect oil, dirt and bacteria and are best
thrown away.

Face powder can do wonders to hold makeup. For
instance, a light dusting over the eyelashes helps your
mascara to thicken. You can also use the powder over
your eyelids to give a base for the eye shadow. In fact,
you can use powder over every special makeup application to help it set and last longer. Lips that are to
be contoured can have a bit of powder applied before
the lip liner and lipstick too. Used properly, powder
can give a finished, flawless look by refining the skin's
texture. A mere touch-up later with face powder can
freshen your face. It will make your makeup last and
look better that much longer.

And even when you want to go natural and choose
to wear no foundation at all, a dusting with a translu-

cent face powder will illuminate your face and give it a finished look, a matte finish, that special effect that only powder can.

CONTOURING

What exactly is contouring? It's the art of knowing where to draw the line. It is really using the art of makeup to its highest potential, of camouflaging and playing up skillfully through the system of darker and lighter colors.

First, light shades will make any feature dominant, while darker shades will make them seem to recede. And so you can take those features that seem larger, more prominent and not in harmony with the rest of your face and subtly shadow them with a darker shade than the rest of your makeup and natural skin tones. Similarly, you will want to learn how to highlight and illuminate those smaller, less obvious areas to bring them forward, and thus more into balance with the rest of your features.

Terminology

You need to know the language to use the tools. There are two terms most used to describe contouring. They are *concealer* and *highlighter*. The concealer is any product that shades or darkens. The highlighter is any product that lightens or plays up. Within the product range are many brands and types of makeup colors and implements—from lip-liner pencils, such as Maybelline and Cover Girl make—to foundation creams from Max Factor to Touch & Glow to Maybelline to Collage—to eye shadows in taupe and brown shades that can be used as well, and which you'll find in every mass-market manufacturer from FlameGlo to Cutex to Maybelline, and so on. Under-eye concealers, eye-pencil crayons in pink, flesh, and darker tones—all of these may serve as either highlighters or concealers, depending on your natural skin color and what area you need to play up or down.

Here is just a brief list of some of the many products you will find at the discount store, the supermarket, the five and dime, in Caldor and K marts and Duane Reade drugstores in the East, in Walgreen's drugstores and, more than likely in the local variety store in your neighborhood too.

Contouring Tools

Cutex Frosty Powder Shadows
Lashbrite Pencils
Angel Face Powder
Cecila's Brush 'n Blush
Tangee Rouge
Fresh 'n Lovely
Maxi Unshine Oil-Free Make-Up
Aziza Soft Stroke Eye Pencils
Maybelline Moisture Whip Creme Blush

Revlon Colorblend Soft Pencils
Constance Carroll Blush Gel
Colláge All Day Blush
Colláge Moisture Base Make-Up
Maybelline Cover Stick (Fair)
FlameGlo Soft 'n Pearly Eye Shadow
Revlon Natural Wonder Foundation Base

The Basics

Now that you know you want to play up certain features and minimize others, what shades should you choose? The basic rule to remember:

For emphasizing, always select shades that are one shade lighter than your foundation makeup, or your natural skin tones if you're not using an all-over foundation base.

For diminishing, select cosmetics that are one or even two shades darker than your foundation, or natural skin tones.

The key technique in applying any contouring makeup over your foundation, or on your skin is to *blend*. There must never be obvious edges.

When? Apply contouring after makeup base, but before you apply blusher, powder, and eye color.

Contouring Cream: How to Use It

When you've decided just where you need some shading, then dot a tiny bit of the shading cream on that specific area of your face that needs correction. Now, using your fingertips, delicately blend the dot until it appears as a natural shadow that has created some hollow area. At first, don't be afraid to overdo the application so you can see just what effect you have achieved. Daytime will require far more subtle contouring, while the dimmer nighttime lighting may call for a bit more exaggerating and intensity.

Using Highlighter

The highlighter is the light shade you'll use to illuminate, to play up a small or special feature. Blushers, light shadows, pink- or flesh-colored pencil crayons, gels, and glosses can all serve in this role of emphasis. And even when you don't want to play up any one feature, consider using some highlighting blusher to give your face an outdoor glow. You might simulate a suntan by applying gel across the bridge of your nose and your cheeks, or try brushing some blusher on the forehead and chin and tip of your nose for a healthy and exciting look.

Practice Makes Perfect

Remember, contouring, especially with darker shades, does take practice. Experiment in private until you're a pro, and then check the final effect in the best possible light. Naturally, daylight is best. Second best is an incandescent, not fluorescent bulb. Look at the total you from every facial view in a mirror to make certain that the effect isn't too harsh or obvious.

Contouring is actually the most fascinating part of applying makeup. It allows you to play a creative role, one that suits only you. It can transform the way you look.

Contouring is also called "boning" the face. For you really are chiseling away, playing up high cheekbones, narrowing a too wide nose, achieving optical illusions by using your face as a surface on which you play with light and dark.

Models and actresses have been trained in contouring and so it is easy for them to use their shading powders and brushes with the quickness and agility of fine artists. Practice is what makes perfect. Once you apply the light and dark touches that best suit your face, you'll begin to notice the compliments you're getting. Soon it will become automatic for you to use a darker shade here and a lighter shade there when applying your makeup.

By the way, a creamy foundation base in a taupe or deep tan shade, depending upon your own natural skin tones, can serve as the most effective all-in-one contouring cream. So can a soft brown eye shadow or a brown crayon pencil. It takes some experimenting to find which medium works the best on your skin, because some creams will be too oily, while some pencils too hard if your skin is on the dry side and you don't blend well. Take time now to play around with many shadows. Soon you'll find the perfect contouring cosmetics that can emphasize your best features and minimize the less attractive ones.

Here's Looking at You

You'll be learning many special tricks for playing up *your* face to best advantage. Here are some simple steps to use in contouring that you can apply to many a situation.

1. First, remember that you must always blend your contouring into your makeup base. There should never be any obvious edges.

2. To thin a wide nose, draw lines down the side with a contouring pencil, then blend well.

3. To lighten a short nose, apply a thin stripe of highlighter down the center.

4. To camouflage a double chin, blend darker color foundation under the chin area.

5. To slenderize a wide face, first frame your face with a darker shade of foundation. Then blend it down the sides of the face from the temples to jawbones, making sure to blend well at the sides and at the hairline.

6. To balance out an uneven lip line, outline and correct the shape with a lip styler-pencil in a

darker color than your lipstick. For the most natural look the line should not extend any farther than the widest section of your nostrils.

7. To shorten a long nose, use dark contour beneath the tip and on the center divider between the nostrils.

8. To play up deep-set eyes, use a highlighter on brow points, being careful to blend into shadow point on lids.

9. To play down shadows under the eyes, use a concealing stick or highlighter or lighter shade of foundation in a careful half-moon contour pattern, before applying overall foundation.

10. If your cheeks are too full, suck in and then apply contour shading in the hollow area that you have created.

Don't forget that most contouring colors should be applied after you have applied your foundation base, and before you have added any blush or final powder to your face. By the way, powder is an excellent technique for softening the overall contouring effects and to hold the look in place. It's a good idea to carry a bit of powder and a puff or two of cotton along to matte out your look later in the day.

Tip: Use an empty spice container that has a sprinkle-hole top for powder. It's easy to carry and to control how much powder you'll want to put on the cotton.

Putting on a New Face

You'll be learning how to contour from each example
that is given in this guidebook and, through your own
experimentation, you will discover which is the best
look for you. But let's take one example of a face and
see just what dimestore products would be used in
creating the best bone structure, the prettiest face one
can, all through the magic of contouring.

The Problem: Female, thirty, with oily skin,
dark circles under her eyes, a too broad forehead,
and an overly wide nose.

The Solution: An oil-control makeup base by
Cover Girl is used to provide good coverage and

a matte finish. A Maybelline cover stick in a fair (lighter than your own skin) shade is applied in the creases, under the eyes to cover shadows, and around the nostrils to camouflage some redness. A soft brown eye shadow by FlameGlo is used at the sides of the forehead to make it seem less wide. A lip color styler-pencil by Aziza is used on the sides of the wide nose to contour and define the bone structure. Her good cheeks are played up with a Colláge cream blusher, and shaded under the bone in a wedge pie shape to show off the good cheekbones. All the contouring colors are blended until there are no sharp edges, and then Angel Face powder is used to achieve a soft, matte finish.

THE NOSE AND CHEEKBONES

Of all of the features of the human face it is actually the nose that has been the most written about. From fable to poetry to love lost and found, from Cyrano de Bergerac to Pinocchio, there have been many tales involving the nose. Today a Streisand may prefer a less-than-perfect one, but still most successful models and many an actress exhibit what might be termed a perfectly straight or "Roman" nose, for in truth, this is still the preferred one in many societies. And so, if your nose is too wide or too hooked or too long or in any way does not fit in proportion to the rest of your face, more than likely you too are not pleased with it.

What to do? Well, short of considering a rhinoplasty operation, you can achieve wondrous results by subtle contouring of the nose through makeup. Harmony and balance will occur when you apply your makeup like an artist, carefully using dark shades to help whatever areas you need to recede to do so, and using lighter shades to bring forth the feature you want to play up. Actually, as we have already learned in the section on contouring, light brings forward and dark helps move back.

So let's look at the art of makeup applied to the nose.

Types of Noses and How to Contour

FOR THE LONG NOSE WITH POINTED TIP: Here, use a lighter shade of foundation straight down the center of the nose, stopping just before the tip. Always leave the end or point darker, or add some dark taupe eyeshadow shade as the concealer. Carefully blend. Product cue: You can use Maybelline's Blooming Brown shadow as the concealer shade, one of Maybelline's soft pink eye-shadow shades as the highlighter shade.

FOR THE LONG NOSE WITH A HIGH BRIDGE: First, choose a darker tone and carefully blend on each side of the nose, right to where the nostrils flare. Product cue: You can choose an eye pencil shade like Aziza's cocoa color and softly stroke it on the sides of your nose, blending well after. Bonne-Bell has a soft taupe shadow in their new Collàge trio eye-shadow collection that may also serve as an ideal concealer shade.

FOR A LARGE AND WIDE NOSE: Choose dark shading on either side of the nostrils, then add a light streak of highlighter in the center of your nose. Then, blend both very well. Product cue: Try colors like Aziza's bisque for the highlighter, and perhaps Aziza's Sand/Driftwood Soft Touch Shadow Duo, for the darker shading. Experiment until you find the shades closest to your own skin tones.

FOR A SHORT, FLAT NOSE: What you want to create is both length and the illusion of height in the contouring, so use a light highlighter generously. First concentrate on the center section, then carefully blend highlighter from flare to flare of each nostril, creating an inverted T contour. Product cue: Here, you might try out Cover Girl's ivory- or fawn-colored shadows.

FOR A WIDE NOSE WITH WIDE NOSTRILS: Highlight the bridge of your nose, to draw the focus to this area, and away from the nostrils. At the nostrils, carefully add some darker tones. Product cues: Try Colláge's apricot blush as the highlighter, using a taupe or cocoa-colored shadow for the concealing shade.

FOR A HOOKED NOSE: Highlighting under the tip of the nose will bring the nose slightly up, while shading the very tip will continue the illusion of shortening and straightening the imbalance. If you also have a bump on your nose, add some more dark shading to that area as well. Blend all the contouring well. Product cues: Try FlameGlo's mocha shadow for the shading areas, and FlameGlo's beige shadow for the highlighting areas.

For a Sharply Upturned-Tip Nose, or one with too Large a Tip: Here, you must darken the area most prominent by shading with a darker tone than the rest of the foundation you apply to your nose. Shade that part of the tip that turns up too much or is too bulbous, then blend carefully. Product cues: Here, you might try Cover Girl's plum eye shadow and use this as the darker contouring shade wherever you want an area to recede.

The next area to the nose that may need attention are your cheeks, their structure and harmony with the rest of your face. You'll find a list of products at the end of this section.

A Cheeky Subject

High cheekbones are an asset in most cases, as are perfectly proportioned cheeks in relation to the rest of your face. Of course, nature endows us as it will, and so we all don't have equally proportioned features. There are gaunt looks from too little fat on the face, and there are also those cheeks that are so round, it's difficult to define them, nor to know just where to apply the rouge. Knowing where to apply cheek color is important. Try this little test:

Look into the mirror. Now, smile as big as you can, forcing yourself to grin as tightly as possible. This will puff out your cheeks. Now, at the very point of the most prominent area of flesh, the most rounded part, this is where you should begin your rouge color. First, apply a dot or two of rouge like Colláge's liquid color or Chap Stick's Moist Glow cream blush, right in the center. Continue to hold that forced smile for a few more minutes to control where the color will go. Blend up and down and out toward the ears, but never any higher than where the top of the ear begins its connection with your head, nor any lower than your earlobes. Now blend well, almost to your hairline, without getting any color on your hair. Allow the edges to fade into the hairline to give yourself a natural glow. Repeat on other side of cheek. Do note that the deepest tone of color should not be so prominent that it stands out from the rest on the cheeks, so soften if you find a harsh blob in the center or near the edges.

Making the Blush Last All Day

From makeup artist and consultant Ted Nadel, who has created makeup for Sassoon Salons, as well as for top fashion models, another great tip: To make your blush last all day, either use a very intense color, well blended, or start with a cream blush like Max Factor's cream blush on top of your foundation, then apply the same tone in a powder blush like Cover Girl's cream powder blush, to set the cream blush. Finish this off with an overall dusting of translucent powder, or just a bit of Johnson's Baby Powder will achieve the same result.

Correcting a Too-Full Face

Here, you need a well-blended application of contour powder blush in a tawny, taupey, or brownish shade. You might try Aziza Natural blush in one of two formulas, either the cream or powder. Or Colláge's All Day Blush, a liquid gel formulation with a rich depth of color. This one comes in apricot, plum, and bronze. Now, brush or apply cream formula to the perimeter of your face, leaving the center area lighter. Follow up to a brushing of the cheek area.

How to Hollow Your Cheekbones

When you want a more dramatic result, hollowing out the cheekbone area may achieve this. Here, you apply a brownish shade of blusher, like Cover Girl's 9 Hour Cheek Color or Ultra Sheen's Powder Blusher, in a deeper-than-your-skin-tone contour color, from brown to taupe to bronze to plum colors, in either a cream or powder formula, to the very center, hollowed-out area of your cheeks, and isolate the shading to that center area only. This is called the "apple" of the cheek, and as we mentioned before, if you smile wide, you'll find that exact apple area. Another way of finding the area is to pucker up and suck your cheeks in; however, you might find yourself with some extra lines that confuse. As in all makeup application, practice makes perfect.

What Colors Are Best for You?

Cheek color can give you the first blush, a healthy look, a dramatic one. It can also make you look silly if it's overdone, or the color is glaringly wrong. What you want to do with rouge is to create warmth, to define or heighten your bone structure. Choosing the wrong shade can confuse the issue. So can using a cream when a powder is best.

How do you know what's best for you? The apply-before-you-buy test works just fine. Go to a big department store like Macy's or the Hecht Co. or a variety store like Woolworth's or M. H. Lamston, anyone that has many cosmetic counters, and spend a few hours trying on the various kinds of cheek rouges. Or use one from the sample display, walk around, and see how long it lasts. We all know about those wonderful looking rouge colors that fade a half hour later. Or the ones that turn dark as your skin gets oily. Experimenting with shades and types that work both with your skin type and coloring is important. You can try on products like Posner's blush powder, Revlon's powder blush, Maybelline's Brush-Blush, Flame-Glo's Blush Stick, Cover Girl's eye shadows and cheek blush, whatever colors will give you the effect you want. Try on many—even if it means a return trip or two. Some quick rules and tips:

1. If you have dry or allergic skin, choose a dry medium rouge. A cream type could cause irritation.

2. If you have oily skin, choose a soft powder type, or those cream rouge types that you have experimented with that won't clog your pores.

3. If you have normal or sensitive skin, you can use either a powder or cream, but be careful of those that are iridescent and may not go on evenly. Again, trial and error works best here.

4. Stay away from metallic, pearlescent, and most iridescent shades of rouge that can create skin irritations and also look overdone, especially in daylight.

5. A deep reddish-brown shade works beautifully on almost all skin tones.

6. If you have very light skin, then choose a pink or light peach color and blend well at the edges.

7. For evening glamour or added drama during the day, try blending two shades like bright red with a deeper bronze or a mauvey rose with a deeper wine shade.

Applying Cheek Color

A fine artist needs fine tools. You will need them too. Of course, there are the wonderful makeup brushes you can purchase. Mod and Aziza are just two brands you'll find in discount stores and dimestores. You might also use good old sterilized cotton as an applicator. In either case, when you're using a powdered rouge, dust lightly, never rubbing the color in.

For cream rouge, your finger is the best applicator.

Be sure to dab on lightly, never pressing or stretching the skin, then gently spread the mixture about.

When you want to achieve depth of color, you'll need to use two shades. When using two colors, first apply the redder color to the cheeks with a wide brush. Then, add the browner rouge tone underneath to define and heighten the look. Smooth and blend with a piece of cotton so that one color bleeds into the other and both soften at the edges. Make sure that the demarcation area doesn't show—that you have brushed the rouge out to the hairline.

As for cuing your cheek color to your lip color, sometimes it works, and sometimes it doesn't. For instance, if you are wearing a peachy-toned rouge, but need a deeper red lipstick to match your dress and your general skin tone, then of course using the same shades or tones of color won't have the proper effect. But where you do want a subtle, all-over color blush to your face, consider using the same red family. Like a bright pink lipstick with a coral rouge. Or a warm plum lipstick with a plum cheek powder.

Finally, remember that any of the rouges that you use for contouring should never be too ashy in tone. Warm plums, burgundy, or warm, deep browns are the best color groups. You'll find these shades made by Cover Girl, Aziza, and Almay, to name just a few.

Other Uses for Cheek Color

Giving your face a healthy all-over blush works well with a full-bodied cheek blush. Dry rouge employed to highlight your temples and the highest part of your eyebrows is a clever trick when you want to widen your face or to focus more attention on this area. And if you don't have the right eye shadow handy, a bit of rose or plum cheek color works just as well on the eyelid. It will give a natural, open glow. Similarly, you can use the deeper burgundy and browns to contour your jawline.

· *Product Cues*

Some other brand-name cheek colors you will find at chain and discount stores: Aziza Natural Lustre blush in cream and powder in bronze, copper, peach, and soft pink tones; Bonne Bell Bronzing Gel to cover your whole face, or just a few areas; Ultra Sheen Powder Blusher in peach and copper tones; Max Factor's fresh blush, cream blush, and powder blush in plums and wines and roses.

THE EYES

Poets have termed them the mirrors of the soul, for our eyes are perhaps the most significant feature of the face. Just think about the world's great beauties: the ancient kohl-rimmed eyes of Cleopatra . . . the luminescent violet eyes of Elizabeth Taylor . . . the doe-shaped seductive ones of Sophia Loren . . . the wide-eyed bright and expressive look of Carol Channing—it's easy to recognize how much of the face is concentrated in the eyes. By playing up your eyes, you will not only enhance their natural beauty through makeup, you will also detract from less attractive features by a properly arched brow and the right emphasis of shadow.

Of course, bright and beautiful eyes reflect both a healthy body and a positive outlook. And so if you're feeling sad or sleepy, your eyes will tell the tale. In those fatigue lines or in under-the-eye shadows, in premature pouches—the eyes' appearance can indicate age and life-style. Of course the wonderful art of makeup practiced through emphasizing and de-emphasizing and correcting can highlight your best features. In your case it may be your eye color, or perhaps long and thick lashes, or the large size of your eyes. Whatever is the magic ingredient that most stands out is what you'll want to enhance, while you'll want to camouflage any problem areas, all through the artful application of makeup.

The Arch of Triumph

Ah, what a difference the properly designed and arched eyebrow can make to the face, for brows are the picture frame of your eyes. Shaping them beautifully and keeping them properly arched and tweezed is an important step in your total eye beauty. Here, then, are easy instructions to follow to achieve a perfectly shaped brow:

1. For easier brow shaping, first test with a pencil to determine the proper place for the brow line to begin. Place a long pencil vertically, so that it touches the side of the nostril and passes over the inner corner of your eyes. Where it hits the brow is the place where the brow line should begin. Now, keeping the end of the pencil at the side of your nose, move the tip over to the outer corner of the eye. (This will indicate just where the brow should end. You should tweeze out only those straggly hairs that fall outside of these two points.)

2. For thinning brows, always tweeze from underneath, one hair at a time, row by row, and gently. Remember, overarching the brows can result in a "surprised" look. Be sure to arch your brow delicately, always starting the shaping at the outer edge of the pupil.

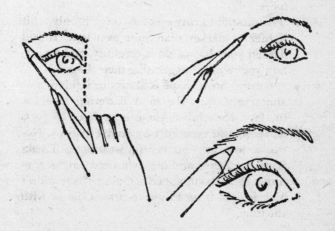

3. An ice cube, gently applied in a piece of gauze or old hankie, will cool the area to be tweezed and make it less sensitive to the tweezing. You'll find lots of cheap but good tweezers in the five and dime.

4. For filling in sparse brows you may use pencil brow coloring, or an eye shadow in powder form. Make short, slim strokes that look most like natural hairs. And, of course, if you can let your brows grow out to a more natural shape, do it.

Slick Tips

● For over-thirties—too-thin brows are aging.
● If you have thick straggly brows that demand tweezing often, you might consider electrolysis, which permanently removes only the excess hairs.
● The most flattering eyebrow color is only a bit lighter or darker than your own hair. If you darken your brows, do it carefully, and be certain you're not exaggerating their shape.
● A natural brow shape is always in fashion, and almost always is the most flattering look for the face. Remember, you can be dated by your makeup, and especially by your eyebrows. Notice a woman who is still wearing a Theda Bara super-thin and highly arched pair of eyebrows. You'll know her age even if she didn't look it, just from this give-away. Change with the times.

Focus on the Eyes:
Special Situations

How to make deep-set eyes appear sparkly and not so sunken? What to do for those close-set eyes? What about eyes that bulge? Here, some special corrective makeup tips for each situation:

FOR WIDER EYES: First, apply a lightener (usually in a lipstick or wand form, one that contains a near-to-the-skin beige or flesh tone, but not a white or very obviously light tone) to the inside corner of your eyes. This lighter shade should almost match your natural skin shade. Now blend against the side of your nose, then extend up and around the eye socket. Add eye shadow, emphasizing the outer third of the brow bone, to give an upward sweep. Keep eyebrows tweezed in a shape that begins no closer than the inside corners of your eyes. This additional space will create a "wide-eyed" appearance.

FOR EYES THAT PROTRUDE: Here you want to create depth by shading the overly prominent eyelid area. Choose deep and intense eye-shadow shades—charcoal, brown, gray, or taupe. Smooth the shadow on the entire lid, and then up to the brow bone and right under the brow line. Of course, you'll want to use a softer shading in the brow bone area, so that there is a soft sweep and you don't end up with a raccoonlike look. Here, a two-tone shadow works just fine. For instance, use the deeper shade of gray on your lid, then the slightly lighter shade on the brow bone and up to the brow. Similarly, you can do this with any two colors of the same family. You might even experiment with mixing two like colors together. Finally, use eyeliner under the outside corner of the lower lashes—this will bring your eye further out and take the focus off the middle area.

FOR DEEP-SET EYES: Hollow-appearing eyes can give a face a washed-out, tired look and a smallish appearance to the eyes, as well as making you look older than you are. What you want to achieve is to bring deep-set eyes forward through the application of more vivid colors. Here, select pale tints almost like a backdrop—applying the lighter-tint shadow across the lid and then up to the brow bone area. A pearly shade that reflects the light is all right, that is, if you're not allergic to the iridescent type.

Since you want to bring the eyes forward, eyeliner, which defines them and gives depth, is out. Instead, consider using globs of mascara, applying more coats than usual, by using face or baby powder, first as a dusting. Of course, an eyelash curler is a must. And false eyelashes, those long, feathered lashes, although not in fashion right now, can do wonders for adding fullness to deep-set eyes. Here, you must tailor-make them for you by trimming them short on the inside section and having flaring fullness at the outside of the lashes.

Finally, putting a dab of a taupe shadow under the lower lashes, only at the outside corner, will continue the illusion.

FOR SMALLISH EYES: Here, the magic of illusion almost works by design. First, you can open up small eyes by applying eye shadow to the lid in the most flattering color for your complexion and hair. Then add a smudged band of brown in the crease of the eye, preferably using a sponge applicator that will give you a nice and smudgy look. Gently fan out the brown shadow so you have no harsh definition of color lines. Finally, add a lighter tone shadow under the curve of the brow bone. You might even put a bit of rouge at the furthest edge to add a rosy hue and add even more interest to the eye area.

Now, use a complementary eyeliner color beginning with a thin line and gradually thickening it as you go over the pupil of the eye. Use lots of mascara, applying it at least twice. As a last step, smudge the same lid color just under the lower lashes of the outside corner.

FOR UNCLEAR OR BLOODSHOT EYES: Of course, see an eye specialist to assure yourself that your eyes and you are in good health. And if fatigue or eyestrain has caused a less than sparkly eye, getting more sleep and proper eye care is the answer. And never, but never, use pink or winey-tone shadows. For makeup: Try a line of blue crayon pencil to pick up and accent the rim of your eyes that will brighten the white section. Of course, apply the blue liner with caution, remembering that subtlety is always the key. Don't apply eyeliner too thickly or extend it beyond the natural eye; the Cleopatra look is out, out, out.

Now, before we give you special makeup looks for the eyes and some specific products you can use, here are some dos and don'ts to study:

The Dos

- Consider an eyelash curler. Mod and Maybelline make them. They can give you longer, fuller-looking eyelashes. When you want to make eyes look larger, upswept lashes that are gently curled will eliminate the casting of shadows by downward-pointing lashes, and therefore will "open-up" the eye. You can purchase a lash curler in any dime or notion store. It should last a lifetime.

- Eye-makeup remover pads are the quickest and easiest way to remove stubborn eye makeup. Waterproof mascara is removed efficiently while the eye area is left moisturized (an important factor, since the skin around the eye is the thinnest and most easily damaged). You'll find lots of brands around, including Andrea Eye QL's thirty-five- and eighty-pad jars. They are packaged in plastic containers that easily travel with you.

- Even cheaper eye makeup remover alternatives are avocado or apricot-kernel oil. Here you condition the lashes and eye areas as you clean them. Remove the mascara by placing a folded tissue between the upper and lower lashes, one that has been saturated in the oil. Never use cotton balls to remove eye makeup—the fibers can catch between lashes and get into the eyes. Baby oil will also do the job in a jiffy.

- If you wear glasses, eye makeup should always

be more pronounced. If you're nearsighted, lenses will make your eyes appear smaller. Use lighter tone shadows to help them appear larger. If you're farsighted, lenses will magnify the eyes, as well as any makeup mistakes. Here, darker shadows work best.

- Precision always counts in making up. Use a magnifying mirror if at all you can, and try to make up in clear, preferably daylight conditions.

- Take into account the dark shadows that appear under the eyes. Regardless of your age they will be visible unless you apply a creamy concealing color—one that is close to your own skin tone—this will minimize any darkness and make your eyes appear larger.

- Always treat the skin about the eyes gently, using moisturizing base and night creams faithfully. Even good old-fashioned Pond's Cold Cream or Dry Skin Cream, or Johnson's Baby Lotion, are good moisturizers you may use about the eye area. And don't forget, a practical jar of petroleum jelly can be used as a lash conditioner—and it works.

- If you have straggly, unshapely eyebrows, consider getting a professional shaping first. Then you can maintain them without ruining the shape by zestily overtweezing.

The Don'ts

- Stay away from heavily frosted shadows. The chemical ingredients that make them sparkle can irritate and are drying. They also can create a crepey look. When you use them, use them sparingly and for special occasions.

- Never pick an eye shadow that is the same color as your eyes, but a muted tone. Remember that most eye shadows are brighter than the iris of the eyes; if they're too bright you'll detract from the total look.

- Stay away from the bright greens and blues as well as any obviously contrasting colors to your complexion and eye and hair color. You don't want that electric blue or lizard green eye look, so any blue or green shade you might choose should be soft, low key, and muted. Remember? If your eye shadow is brighter than your eyes, people will be talking to your eyelids and not to you.

- Stay away from white and off-white as highlighters. They don't highlight, but stand out. What you want is a soft and a subtle effect. Makeup artist Ted Nadel always uses a pink crayon pencil and says that you should stay close to your own skin tones in any highlighters or cover-up products.

- If you have puffy lids or a pronounced brow area, stay away from bright shades. All light colors bring the features forward and so the problem area will only be more exaggerated.

- When eyes are surrounded by darkish circles, don't choose any muddy, green, or dark ashy-brown shadows. They will only extend the area of discoloration.

- Don't use fiber-filled mascara products, especially if you wear contact lenses, for the eyes can become irritated. Also, fiber-filled mascara tends to dry. Better to powder lashes first, then apply regular mascara.

Implements

The best artist uses the best tools, and tools are what you need in applying eye makeup. Ted Nadel suggests that disposable sponge applicators are the best. He explains that some eye shadows are bright and intense in the container, but are dull and flaky when applied with a brush. Better to use a sponge applicator, which you may purchase separately at the dimestore, or as part of a makeup application kit. There are a number of inexpensive brushes and applicators you may purchase, like the one made by Andrea or Mod. You may also purchase an artist's flat-tipped sable brush for applying eye shadow. Even dry eye shadow goes on better and remains longer if you'll apply it with brush dipped into a small container of water.

Don't forget a good magnifying mirror, which is an important investment in your entire makeup performance, and if you don't have good light, then perhaps you'd like to invest in one of those lighted makeup mirrors.

Matching Colors

Probably one of the most vital ingredients in a proper makeup scheme is using the correct colors. And this means not only mascara, which can be purchased in more than basic black and brown, but eyeliner pencils, shadows, and concealing creams. Manufacturers are constantly coming out with a new color collection of makeups, which can be confusing. After all, they're doing it to interest the consumer in purchasing another product. At least twice yearly companies like Maybelline introduce yet another line of colors through an all-out advertising campaign. Don't just buy to buy—but buy what will look pretty and refreshing. Stay within the tones that you already know work, no matter how terrific the latest "Golddigger Frost" or "Blooming Blue" may be. It's not so terrific if it's the wrong color for you.

Here are color cues of some of the best shades of eye shadow, pencil, and eyeliners to use, some of the mascara tones, and after, a list of the product types you will find at the discount store, dimestore, and supermarket.

BROWN EYES. You may choose any shade, as long as it's not overly bright, and if it enhances your natural coloring.

GREEN EYES. Plum, taupe, brown, muted blue, navy blue, deep turquoise, olive, and some blue/greens work best.

BLUE EYES. Charcoal, gray, plum, violet, brown, muted green and muted turquoise, navy, are best.

HAZEL EYES. Plum, brown, taupe, muted green, some violets, blue, and turquoise do well.

Product Cues

For mascara, eye crayon pencils, shadows, creams, makeup brushes, and removal pads and lotions too, you'll find a wealth of colors, exciting new pencils, every implement you need in the supermarket, the five and dime, the local chain and discount store. Here are some of the save-money products available to help you make up your eyes:

From Maybelline you'll find products like the Blooming Colors Powder Shadow Collection—four eye-shadow shades in one container, six different combinations to choose from, including frosts, mattes, and the Blooming Blues and Browns. There are also the mascaras, including Maybelline's Comb-On, their Cake Mascara, and the Ultra-Lash Mascara. For the eyeliners by Maybelline you'll find an Automatic Overliner/Underliner as well as a Waterproof Ultra-Liner. There are also eyebrow tweezers in a straight or slant style, the automatic eyebrow pencils, the twin pack eyebrow pencil, and of course a really big assortment of colored Eye Color Styler-Pencils, as well as the new Double Barreled Color Eye Pencil.

Max Factor makes a line of makeup products that are sold in discount stores and dimestores, like their Maxi-Lash Mascara and the Maxi cream and powder blushes, as well as many shades of eye color pencils for you to use.

Bonne Bell has a new line of makeup called "Colláge." There are some excellent eye makeup products here too. For instance, the Collàge eye-shadow collection is actually a trio powder. Instead of the traditional light-medium-dark tones of the same shade, primary and secondary colors are used with a universal highlighting shade. Here, the back of the card is thoughtfully printed to tell you what goes best with what. Collàge also has a slim Precision Eye Pencil in three soft kohl shades, as well as a Lash Conditioning Mascara.

Aziza offers Soft Stroke Eye Pencils that are quick, convenient, and easy to use. Here you can accent for liner or do a brow-to-lash shadow and contour job. The formula is creamy, easy to apply and handle.

Cover Girl has a wide array of eye shadows and mascaras and pencils including pressed powder shadows, moist eye shadows, and cream-on shadows. Their Thick Lash Mascara and Professional Mascara are both bargain finds that do the job too. There is also a cream-on shadow with wand, soft liner, brow liner, and pencils, and a long and lush mascara that you'll find at the local discount, chain and dime stores in your area.

Revlon's Natural Wonder product line is sold in supermarkets. You'll find a display of eye pencils, shadows, and mascaras for the high-fashion eye look. Revlon also makes products like their Big Lash mascara and eye wear that you'll find in the local notion and dimestore branches.

FlameGlo is another product brand widely sold in discount stores and dimestores. Here you'll find duo eye-shadow kits, natural eyelashes, Soft Eyes Night Sparklers, Soft 'n Pearly Eye Shadows, Hours Longer Mascara, and many other bargain beauty finds.

Mod's Curl-Up Lash Curler and a five-brush Applicator Collection can be found in many chain stores, as well as the five and dime.

Johnson's has a number of products that help with eye care and makeup, including Johnson's cotton swabs, Baby Oil, Baby Powder, Baby Lotion.

Nu-Masca is a brand name—found in dimestores—that carries eye shadows, eye-shadow sticks, an inexpensive Let's Get Fresh eye pencil, and an Eye Shadow Theatre kit in a variety of pretty shades.

Of course, these aren't all. Each store has specials and special brands and many carry their own name collections of makeup that are just as cheap as the more expensive "designer" names are. In most cases, house brands are your best buys of all. Look for them first.

The Magic of Mascara

No-smudge, of course. From Maybelline's Great-Lash to FlameGlo's Lush Lash Mascara to Cover Girl's Professional Mascara, there are a wonderful variety of eyelash-lengthening mascaras to choose from, and quite a few colors too. Like navy blue or purple or brown/black, as well as black and browns, you can add color and definition through the lashes by applying a dramatic shade. There are comb-ons and brush-on wands, cake and brush application styles, liquid-in-the-bottle types—and as we already have discussed, many brands to choose from.

What you want to do is to make sure that even if

you're not wearing much shadow, that you get in the habit of using mascara on a daily basis. For there is really nothing more lacking than a woman who has foundation, cheek rouge, lipstick, and pale, non-mascaraed eyes. Mascara is the most important dressing for your eyes, especially if you have fine and light-colored lashes. You should also choose a waterproof mascara so your mascara won't smudge during the long day's wearing.

When applying mascara, advises Ted Nadel, always do the bottom lashes first. When looking up (for that's the position your eyes should be in), carefully apply the mascara to the lower set of lashes, always applying it from above. When you're applying mascara on the upper eyelashes, reverse, and begin from underneath the lash area. To avoid mascara smudges, tilt your head back as you stroke on the color. You might also fold a tissue and hold it near the lashes to catch any excess color. A cotton tip, dipped in water, will remove any smears if they occur.

To prevent lashes from clumping, wipe off any excess mascara on the applicator before using it. An old, clean mascara brush helps separate the lashes if you still find they're sticky. And if your lashes are thin, or you just want a nice and thicker look, dust first with face or baby powder, then apply a coat of mascara.

Just as important as using mascara is removing it at day's end. You may use apricot or avocado oil, baby oil, even Pond's Cold Cream or a jar of White Rose Makeup Remover Petroleum Jelly will do. A big pound jar of the petroleum jelly lasts a long, long time and can be found in many five and dime and discount stores. And do remember, use tissue, not cotton, when removing makeup from the eye area.

Making More of Your Eyes

Learning by practice helps. Here are two simple eye-makeup ideas you can imitate and see how they do for you.

USING BLUSH. Here, bring the blush you would use on your cheekbones on the lid and browbone above the eye. This will let the eye color really stand out. It is a fresh-for-spring-and-summer look when you don't want a heavy, complicated makeup look. You may use a deeper shade on the lid so when the eyes are open, the shadow doesn't obtrude.

ONE COLOR PINK LOOK. Here you highlight with a pink pressed powder, and use it not only on the lid but under the brow and over to the black pencil at the corner. First, use a thin, soft black pencil to line the lower lashes. Then, brush a pink iridescent powder over the pencil on the outer crease and under the lower lashes. Blend. Then use black pencil to line the upper lashes, outer corner, and outer crease. Blend. Finish up with mascara.

Cheap Tricks

We've all seen them—models, actresses, and everyday women, who have before-and-after photos taken of a makeup session. Just what makes the "after" so dramatically different and beautiful? Do makeup artists have special hints that we can apply at home? Of course there are, just like the ones Ted Nadel has given us. Here, a compendium of other professional tips that you can adapt to your own needs and situations. They're the tops in tips from pros that will help you use the reasonably priced cosmetics to do just as great a job as the higher priced ones can do; all it takes is a bit of practice and patience.

- Begin eye shadow about a quarter inch above the lash line, keeping the area just above the lashes bare of color. This makes for a very sensual eye. You can also put a bit of petroleum jelly, or even a touch of pale gold or silver shadow there.

- Blend several colors of eye shadow for more depth. Experiment with those eye trio kits and different colors until you get an individual blend that is best and most dramatic for you.

- Apply mascara with the tip of the brush only. Hold it almost vertically to separate the lashes. For a really dramatic doing, apply many thin coats, so each one dries without caking.

- Imagine vertical lines passing through the center of the eyes. All makeup, except lipstick, goes outside those lines.

- Brown and blue, mixed together, create a muted eye-shadow shade that is usually flattering to everyone.

- Heavier eyeliner makes eyes appear smaller. If you use liner, smudge it with your finger so it's blurry and looks left over from yesterday. It's also sexier that way.

- Don't slant shadow or liner upward in a hard pronounced line. It's dated and makes for an unattractive profile.
- If your eyebrows are too dark, rub a bit of foundation into them. Brows should only be a shade or two lighter or darker than the lashes. If you have really thin or skimpy brows, fill in with a soft brow powder. Don't use an eyebrow pencil, which will give you a Groucho Marx result. It's too hard on light or thin eyebrows.
- When making up your eyes, always drop your mouth open. In this manner you'll avoid raising your eyebrows and creating endless and needless wrinkles on your forehead.
- Curl lashes only if they're short and grow straight out or down. Overcurling results in the cutesy Betty Boop look, as well as lash breakage.
- To reach the inner-eye corner with powder, fold a small powder puff in half and use just the folded edge. For applying concealer under or in corners of the eyes, use a slim, tapered brush or sponge applicator, blending the lightener in a small triangle from the inner corner to the center of the eye, then downward.
- Application of face or baby powder on top of the first application of eye shadow, then reapplying the shadow, will help it set.

For Lasses Who Wear Glasses

Here is a makeover by Ted Nadel that you can duplicate to play up your eyes under glasses:

STEP 1. Use a moisturizing base, then translucent powder to set.

STEP 2. Using a C stroke, which is the manner to best apply a regular blush powder about the eye area, extend the blush from the inner corner of the eye out to the far corner of the eyebrows. This enlarges a small eye and gives definition under the glasses.

STEP 3. Take a blending brush and using a soft eye crayon as a cream shadow, apply well to the upper lid of the eye, then finish off with powder to set.

STEP 4. Using a sparkling highlighter shade, or a salmony-fleshy toned colored pencil, add more color to the upper lid, blending all over.

STEP 5. Use a black kohl pencil to line both the upper and lower lids.

STEP 6. Use lots of mascara, in one or two coat applications.

STEP 7. Using the same flesh-toned (a tea rose shade) eye color pencil, erase any problems about the eyes, smudges, or overdone color.

STEP 8. Apply lipstick, using a lip pencil liner to outline the lips. You can define and make up for nature's mistakes by using the flesh-toned pencil to erase all the outer edge smears and to blend.

STEP 9. Rouge well under the cheekbones.

STEP 10. Dab a bit of gold highlighter to the best parts of your face, just to add a little extra light.

STEP 11. Dust off the face with translucent or baby powder, using a big soft brush.

STEP 12. Put on your glasses and just look. Don't you look terrific?

Extra Economy Tips

● Brush your eyebrows with a "retired" toothbrush. They need care, too. Brush against the growth pattern, then straight up, and finally, level them at the ends into a flattering arch.

- Petroleum jelly can be a boon when you forget eye makeup and need a quick picker-upper when you're traveling or are away. Put a bit in an empty pill container to toss into your purse and use as a substitute whenever the need arises —to add gleam to lids and to lashes. By the way, a final touch of jelly will make straggly eyebrow hairs stay in place.

Color Palette

I have already suggested basic color combinations earlier on in this chapter. Individual complexion, hair color, eyes, and the time of the year, as well as time of day and occasion are all other factors in just what colors to use. Here then is an in-depth outline color wheel of hair shades and eye colors and what eye makeup colors usually go best with each.

Of course, you should experiment, mixing shades, playing up some colors, using others for night or dress-up moods. This book gives you the basic rules and the economy products to do the professional job with. It should inspire you to practice and find your very own special makeup looks. Don't be afraid to try out a shade that matches your eye color, or a summer tan, or even a dynamite dress. Just be sure that the colors are complimentary to you, that they don't stand apart but give you an overall, a total beauty look. Remember, you want comments that are compliments, that say *you* look beautiful, not your eye makeup, nor your dress.

Brownettes with brown eyes—Use brown or plum or mauve shadows; brown mascara; brown on brows.

Brownettes with blue eyes—Use violet, navy, muted green, or blue shadow; black mascara; palest color for eyebrows.

Blondes with blue eyes—Use lilac, mauve, soft rose, or gray shadows; brown mascara; palest color for eyebrows.

Blondes with brown eyes—Use brighter blue shadow, mauves, and taupes; black mascara; pale gray on brows.

Brunettes with brown eyes—Use taupe, deep brown, sand, or plum shadow; dark-brown mascara; soft brown for brows.

Brunettes with blue eyes—Use navy, violet, moss green, muted blue, or gray shadow; black mascara; dark brown on brows.

Brunettes with hazel eyes—Use plums, mauves, hunter green, moss green, blue/green, browns, and violets; black mascara; dark brown on brows.

Redheads with brown eyes—Use brown, violet, muted or moss green shadow; violet shadow if you're light complexioned and have small eyes; brown mascara; pale or natural brow color.

Redheads with blue eyes—Use navy, muted blue, gray, or soft mauve shadows; brown mascara; pale or natural brow color.

Gray hair with blue eyes—Use sand, taupe, or plum/violet shadow; black mascara; gray on brows.

Black hair with brown eyes—Use violet or deep gray or plum shadow; black or dark brown mascara; dark brown on brows.

Black hair with blue eyes—Use lavender, slate gray, or navy shadows; black mascara; dark brown on brows.

What about unusual eye colors? If you have violet, green, gray eyes, then pick a complementary shadow to play up your exceptional eyes. Especially pretty is the use of a pencil crayon (in the same color as your eyes) as an under-eye liner; this picks up and plays to your eye color. You might also use an unusual color mascara—purple with gray or violet eyes, navy with green or violet eyes. And a tip for all—brown or deep plum shadow can work well for almost everyone. These shades don't distract by being too obvious and work wonders when you want to contour and reshape. Also, your blusher can be used in a pinch to highlight above the eye, on the brow bone, and even as shadow, unless you have blotchy skin and any red in your eyes. In most cases, just a bit of color will pick up the light and add focus to the feature by dusting with a tawny or a similar soft peach shade.

THE MOUTH

Emphasizing and de-emphasizing the lips will shape your mouth to match your face. How? Practice by outlining your lips with a soft brown shade of pencil. You can try Aziza or Maybelline eye pencil crayons for this purpose. Use these rules:

1. If your mouth is small, line the upper and lower indentations of the mouth with lip pencil or brush, by going a bit over the edge of the lips to increase the area. Then fill in the lips with the shiniest gloss, adding an even shinier shade of gloss or a pink pencil color right in the center of the lower lip.

2. If your mouth is large, line it inside the natural lip line, using a lip brush. Then fill in with a matching shade of lipstick, or perhaps a deeper shade on the lower lip. Applying more color on the bottom lip also gives an illusion of less fullness.

Lip Trips: How to Use Color and Gloss

Lip colors, like all cosmetics, work best when you employ them to create a variety of looks. For instance, you may want just a little bit of lip gloss on some occasions, while on others you just wouldn't dream of going out without a drop-dead all-out color plus shine.

Lipsticks and glosses can do a lot more than just cover your mouth. They keep your lips fresh and moist looking and can help protect against the elements—sun, wind, chapping. You can even use them to make your mouth look smaller or larger, to give a clearer shape and prettier curves.

Just about every manufacturer offers lipsticks, lip

glosses, and shines in dimestore and discount varieties. Maybelline has a new Ultra-Slim Lipstick that is sleek and helps you apply a thin dollop where you need it, in this manner controlling just how much goes on. Of course, you'll find lots of lip-coloring pencils that shape and color in one single stroke. Aziza has a wide array of lip pencils in shades like natural, copperwood, ginger, honey red, plum wine, and bronze, so you see there is much versatility available for defining and outlining and coloring the mouth. There are also the lip glosses—some, by FlameGlo and Maybelline, contain conditioners—special emollients and oils to promote maximum moisturizing. They can help keep your lips well conditioned.

Bonne Bell offers long-lasting lip colors, Good Nature Lip Gloss, Lip Glow, and a group of Lip Smackers—sun-screen, moisture-shine lip gloss in a stick form that comes in wild flavors—everything from strawberry to green apple to orange chocolate. In the Colláge line of lipsticks by Bonne Bell, there are six color-cued shades from which to choose. And so on. From Cutex to Maxi by Max Factor to Cover Girl's lip softener lipstick line to Hazel Bishop's complete lipstick line—every major cosmetic maker has at least one lipstick and one gloss, or liquid lipstick in a wand, in the line, so go on and try on some exciting new colors and see just what you like.

Apply Before You Buy

There are many lipstick testers in stores like Walgreen's, Genovese, Caldor, and K mart, in almost any chain drug outlet and even in small drugstores, available so you can afford to try on the lipstick shade and make sure that it's right for you. First, always clean the lipstick tester. Ask the sales clerk for a tissue if you haven't one. Then when you try on the shade, check it in daylight. Give the lipstick time to turn too orange or too blue. If it does, you know it doesn't have any staying power for you, that more than likely, it is combining with your natural oils to create an off color. If it is satisfactory, then you can feel secure in making the purchase. Remember, the color in the tube is never the color on you.

Lip Tips

- Always use gloss, whether you're wearing lipstick or not. It creates extra shine and lubrication. To help your lipstick from changing color on your lips, apply gloss first, then lip color.
- Emphasize a pretty mouth with a dab of white highlighter. You might try a Cutex white pencil. Apply in the cleft above your upper lip, and then just under the middle of the lower one. Of course, blend the white spot so that it isn't overly obvious.
- Outline your lips with a lip brush by Mod or a lip color pencil made by Aziza or Maybelline, for a clearer definition. Then fill in by using the same brush to help the color set and stay on longer.
- De-emphasize too-full lips by first outlining with a brown pencil. Follow the natural line inside your own lip line. Add a darker color to the bottom lip to make the lip recede.

Tricks of the Trade

From makeup artist Ted Nadel come some professional tips he uses to camouflage problems of the mouth.

1. For lips that have creases that create runny, smeary lines: stop running lipstick by powdering a fairly heavy pressed powder around and onto the lip area. Then line the lips and blend the liner at the edges, avoiding a definite pencil line.

2. Inexpensive, drier-formula lipsticks are the best for running lipstick problems. The color will sit longer. If the look is too dry or cracky, add a touch of gloss to the lower center of the lip.

3. Always buy a stiff lip brush for more control. Work with the side of the brush for a pencil-thin outline. This will avoid sloppy lip outlines, gooey lipstick.

Lip-Color Guide

Lip color should give a sense of proportion to your face by relating properly to your eye color. A new lip color can update your look almost instantly; however, be careful not to match the color to a dress when it might clash with your eye makeup, your foundation, your skin tone. The shade and sheen should balance with your entire makeup look. If you want to mix and match, then match your lip color to your hair and eyes, not your outfit. Here are some basic rules to follow in choosing colors that complement each other:

Hair and Eye Color:	Complementary lip colors:
Redhead/blue or brown eyes	Peach, coral, deep orange, clear red
Blond/blue or lilac eyes	Raspberry, soft pink, hot pink
Blond/brown eyes	Plum, wine, deep berry, mocha
Brunette/brown eyes	Copper, plum frost, berry, wild fuchsia
Brunette / blue or green eyes	Clear red, plum, wine, mocha, hot pink
Black/black or brown eyes	Mahogany, copper, deep pink, coral, plum frost
Black/blue eyes	Cherry red, frosted pink, coffee, plum, coral

If your lips have too much natural color or if they are too dark in tone, use a foundation base or a bit of under-cover eye stick to fill in before applying the lip color with a brush.

A Girl's Best Friend

Is the lipbrush. If you have never used one, you don't know what you're missing. You can easily pick up a dimestore lipbrush, made by Mod or another mass manufacturer, or try a thin sable artist's watercolor brush. The idea: get used to applying lipstick with a brush to assure longer lasting color. It also gives you more control and precision in applying.

How to use a lipbrush? First, outline the lips with the line you want to use to best emphasize or de-emphasize the area. Now, gently round the corners using the brush on the edge, only. A brush offers control, accuracy. You can correct a lip line easily, as well as blending one shade into another. Be sure that you pick up enough color on the brush by brushing it back and forth against the lipstick generously. After you've applied, tissue off any excess lipstick from the brush. Every so often, for sanitary reasons, dip it into a bottle of alcohol (the seventy percent kind). Allow the brush to dry well before using again.

Liquid Lipsticks

Liquid lipstick packaged in a tube or wand isn't really that new. They were introduced a long while ago, had a wave of popularity, then waned. Today most manufacturers are producing excellent liquid lipsticks—from Maybelline's entire line of glossy lip colors that come in convenient tubes with brush applicator or their kissing slicks—to FlameGlo's roll-on gloss, you'll find lipstick colors that come in a variety of containers and packages at the dimestore and chain store. Most have a creamy, shiny formula and come in leakproof automatic containers much like the old roll-on mascara packages. What is handy about liquid lipstick is you can use it as a top gloss, over another color to add luster, or to freshen up later.

Remember, the mouth can be the most desirable

feature of the face. Too much lipstick, a sloppy line, gooey gloss, and heavy, dark colors can make you look bizarre. You should create a natural, pretty lip line, and then, except for some public touch-ups, leave well enough alone. Too much lipstick will take away from the total you. A dab of gloss later will often do.

Lips in the Sun

Baring your sensitive lips to the harsh sun can do damage, since there are no oil glands within the lip area to fight the parch and the harmful rays. It makes sense to treat your lips separately from the rest of the face. First try a coating of zinc oxide, that thick white ointment you can pick up in any drugstore. Or if you think creamy ointments like Nivea Skin Oil or Noxzema are enough, then use these, reapplying whenever you need to. Then there are the new lipsticks that contain sunscreens in them. Whatever products you decide to use—use them. In this case bare is bad and you should always keep some moisturizing product on your mouth.

Cheap Tricks

Good old petroleum jelly is a great lip glosser. So is old-fashioned Crisco or any good cooking or salad oil. Put a dab in an old pill container and carry it along with you for use at the beach, on trips, for any emergency. And of course, a dollop of old-fashioned honey can make a lip-smacking lip-licking salve.

When you haven't lipstick handy, cheek blusher will do. Sometimes the same brown tones on cheeks and lips work well in pulling the face together.

Keep dental floss in your cosmetics kit. The prettiest smile in the world isn't pretty if you have particles in your teeth. Similarly, white-as-can-be teeth complements pretty lips, so brush often and well. If you have yellowing teeth, try lemon to bleach them, and avoid any lip colors that have too much orange in them. Orange is never a flattering shade to any skin tone.

Avoid a stiff upper lip. If you're pouting you'll look uptight or stiff, and all the lipstick in the world won't do you a bit of good. Try smiling.

MAKEUP SUMMARY

The Summing Up

You've learned the basics, what to put on and where and why. Practicing now with your mirror and trying out the products you'll find that do the job are the next steps. But what about making the look last? After all, if you spend a half hour putting on your face, you should expect that it will last all day long. And night.

Everything looked just right when you left the house yesterday—lipstick, blusher, mascara, eye shadow. But by lunchtime a glance in the mirror showed a washed-out you—it looks as though you're not wearing any makeup at all. No, you needn't reapply everything two or three times a day. What you need to learn are the basics, those secrets for making your makeup stay.

Foundation

Make certain that your face is properly cleaned, toned, and moisturized before applying the foundation. This means cleansing with soap and water, or whatever liquid cleanser you use, then dabbing astringent on those areas of your face that tend to be oily, while using moisturizer on the areas that tend toward dryness.

Very oily faces will benefit from using an oil-reducing foundation like those made by Cover Girl and Maybelline. You might also carry some of those oil-blotting papers along. Aziza makes them in an easy carry pouch.

Before applying foundation, use a concealer by Maybelline or Revlon's Natural Wonder line, on under-eye circles, red, blotchy areas, dark spots, and any blemishes. Pat it on gently with your fingertips, or if you're working with a very small area, try to use a fine cosmetic applicator.

It helps to use a dampened sponge when applying foundation. It will spread your makeup on smoothly and evenly, and you can always pick up excess foundation with a clean area of the sponge. Use light, quick strokes, blending the makeup over but not into the skin. Use less foundation on a sponge than you would

on your fingers—your fingers absorb a lot of the makeup, the sponge very little.

If you find you need more coverage in a particular spot, dab some extra foundation on it lightly with your fingertips and allow to dry. A final dusting of translucent powder by Max Factor or even Johnson's Baby Powder, or whatever shade best matches your skin tones, is all you need for a perfect base that should last all day and into the evening.

Of course you may want to refresh the oilier areas of your face—nose and chin and forehead. The best way to do this is to mix a bit of foundation with face powder and carry this heavier mixture along in an empty container that you can use to dab about on those areas where the makeup tends to wash away. A fresh dusting of face powder often is all that is needed, but it helps if you're planning on a long day and evening out to have the mini-base with you as well.

Eye Makeup

The first trick to keeping your eye makeup on all day is to make sure you cover your lids with foundation before applying any eye makeup. This gives the shadow a base to cling to and also helps the color look truer. Make sure you cover all the tiny veins that line your lids and the inner corner of your eyes.

Once you've decided what color eye shadow—like FlameGlo, Cover Girl, or the Colláge color-cued products—you're going to wear, choose an eye pencil crayon, like those made by Aziza or Maybelline, in the same color (or a complementary color—like a brown pencil with taupe shadow) and line your eyes. Large eyes look best lined all around; smaller eyes need liner on the outer half only.

Blend the pencil with your finger or a cotton swab until the line smudges into a feathery look. Now, using a sponge-tipped applicator, apply your shadow, blending it in well. Always apply just a little bit more than you want to wear; your skin will absorb some of the color. Don't worry about it appearing too dark. It will fade in about an hour to exactly the shade you wanted in the first place. You could do your makeup an hour earlier than you expect to go out, if you're concerned about looking too made up.

Mascara comes last. The longest-lasting mascara is really the cake variety, which you mix with water and apply with a brush. Cake mascaras also don't smudge as easily during the day because they don't have an oil base to mix with the oils in your skin. Use two applications of mascara, removing any excess gently with your fingertips or a comb or the edge of a cotton swab. Or if you want to emulate the cake finish, try using a coat of talcum powder before applying liquid mascara, then coating again, then another layer of mascara. Finally, a little powder under the eye will further prevent smudging and smearing during the day.

Blusher

Blusher will last the longest if you'll use both a cream and a powder type. First, apply the cream, blending it in with a sponge or your fingertips. Give it a couple of minutes to sink in, then apply powder blush over it with quick, light strokes. Again, use more color than you need—at least half of it is going to fade away inside of an hour after application. Use the blusher wherever you need it, even the tip of your nose for a sun-kissed look, even in winter.

Lipstick

This is the one cosmetic most of us can't keep on, and it's obvious why. We do use our mouths all day, from drinking water, to dining, to smoking, and so on. After a meal most of your lipstick will be gone. But you can minimize the problem by following a few simple rules: Get out of the habit of licking your lips during the day, learn to cut fruit up in pieces before eating it (biting into an apple will take just about all of your lipstick off in one fell swoop), and do use a straw when you're sipping on those No-Cal liquids. And of course, don't nibble on pencils, pens, or chew on your fingernails.

Lipstick that is well applied in the morning could last through your lunch, and another application could just about make it through dinner. How? In the morning cover your lips with foundation, the same that you use on the rest of your face. Then, using a lipbrush and lipstick, or using a lip-liner pencil, carefully outline your lips, following the natural contours. (Or if you need contouring and correction, follow the instructions in the chapter on the mouth.) If you use a pencil, smudge the line lightly with your finger so it doesn't look harsh and unnatural. Then fill in with lipstick. Using a lipbrush to fill in will give you the greatest amount of color and coverage and you'll be able to fill in the corners without smudging outside of your natural lip line. Finish with gloss if you like a shiny look.

A final touch for setting all of your face makeup: Use a fine spray bottle filled with mineral water. Keep it in the fridge so that it's fresh and cool. Spray a fine mist over your face and allow it to dry. It will seal your makeup and keep it looking fresher all day.

Final Tips

The most perfect makeup can be spoiled if you aren't careful. Here are some special things you can do to take care, to become more aware of how to keep you looking the way you want to.

- Put makeup on after you've gotten dressed. If you're afraid of spilling some on your clothes, wrap a towel around your shoulders.

- If it's too late and you've already put your makeup on, drape a silk scarf over your head before pulling on any dress or sweater. Press your lips together to keep from smearing lipstick on your garments.

- Try not to touch your face with your hands during the day. Leaning with one hand under your chin is preferable, if you must lean at all. But avoid fidgeting with your hair or your face. Every time you touch your face, you'll smudge your makeup. Besides, it makes you look fidgety.

- To prevent makeup from getting into your hair while you are applying it, cover your hair with a scarf or even a shower cap.

- On rainy days wear as much waterproof makeup—like waterproof mascara and powder rouge—as your skin can take. Be sure to keep a rain hat with a brim over your face when it's really pouring and you must go out.
- A quick puff of powder can do wonders to remove a shine on your face. Don't travel without a bit of powder for this use.

CHAPTER V

Hands and Feet

Hand Signals

How exactly do our nails grow? From under the skin and behind the cuticle. The embryo nail actually consists of gellike cells, which harden and form the nail plate when they reach the air. As more and more embryo cells are formed, slowly the nail plate is pushed along the nail bed toward the fingertip. Nails, like hair, are really dead matter, and like hair are made of a similar substance, keratin. Some nails, like hair, are thicker than others. Some of us are born with stronger nails and hair. Nutrition, how we care for them, can also play a role in having beautiful hands and nails. Proper filing and polish can actually strengthen the nail.

Your nail know-how should also concern your toenails. Pretty feet, properly pedicured and cared for, are as feminine and important as hands that have a good manicure. And you don't have to spend a small fortune on either professional manicures or pedicures to have pretty, healthy-looking nails on your hands and your feet. Learning the basics of giving yourself a good manicure and pedicure are important. So will using the right tools. First the general rules:

The Know-Hows:

- Before manicuring the nails, you should make sure your hands are not only clean, but are free of any kind of hand-lotion film, which can affect the application of nail color.

- Always shape nails with an emery board. You'll find an abundance of them at your local Woolworth's or K mart stores. A clipper or pair of scissors tend to separate the nail layers, leading to splits and breaks. File in one direction only—if you saw back and forth you'll also weaken and split the nail.

- Always file from the outer corner in. Don't attempt to do both sides of the nail together, but file one side, then the other, always moving toward the middle.

- Always polish your handiest hand first; you'll be less likely to smudge these nails while you're polishing the other hand. Start with the thumbnail, which usually takes longer to dry.

- In order to protect nails from ripping at the corners, and also to improve the wear of nail color, brush nail polish on the underneath part of the nail that extends from the finger.

- To make nail color go further, and also to prevent your nails from turning yellow, use a base coat. It dries quickly and is designed to make the nail polish adhere to it. Then, after this, place two thin coats of the nail polish. Wait a few moments, then apply a top coat. Finally, brush on top coat of a colorless sealer; the plasticizers in the sealer will give flexibility as well as longer life.

- Never trim your cuticles. Trimming only toughens this dead skin and encourages hangnails and raggedy edges. Instead push gently back every day, and use cream if you tend to have very dry cuticles. You may snip away at hangnails if you must, but be careful or you'll have an infection.

- Like food, nail color in the bottle goes bad after a while. Throw out after about three years, if you still have any left in the bottle.

- If you live in a warm climate, refrigerating nail polish will keep it freshest and help in the application.

The Basic Implements for a Manicure

You'll find row upon row of nail files, emery boards, cuticle scissors, nail nippers, and such in the dime-stores and discount stores. The choices are wide and many—from Cutex to Maybelline to Andrea to Max Factor—there are a host of nail-care helpers. Here is just a partial list of the products you'll find on the market:

Product Cues
Max Factor Nail Guard

Max Factor Nail Wrap Kit
Cutex Nail Strengthener
Andrea Nail Polish Remover Pads
Andrea Nail Repair and Wrap Kit
Cutex Creamy Cuticle Remover Kit
Courtesy Polish Remover
Revlon Nail Hardener
Revlon Super Nails
Maybelline Cuticle Remover
Sally Hansen Nail Finisher
Sally Hansen Buffing Kit
Sally Hansen Nail Treatment

As for nail polishes, well, the world is your oyster. From Maybelline to Cutex to Cover Girl to Andrea to Posner to Constance Carroll to Sally Hansen to Honey & Spice to Revlon to Hazel Bishop to Fabergé, you'll find cream enamels, fillers and base coats, iridescent shades, pales, brights, a true rainbow of nail-polish colors to pretty up your hands and your feet. With all of these choices you can easily find just the right color and type of polish to fit your mood and personality. How to apply it? Read on.

How to Give Yourself a Manicure

Before you begin, check your supplies. Have everything arranged beforehand, so you won't find yourself getting up halfway through the manicure to get a piece of pumice or a top coat, and then smudging your nails.

What you'll need: Cotton swabs, an emery board, or-

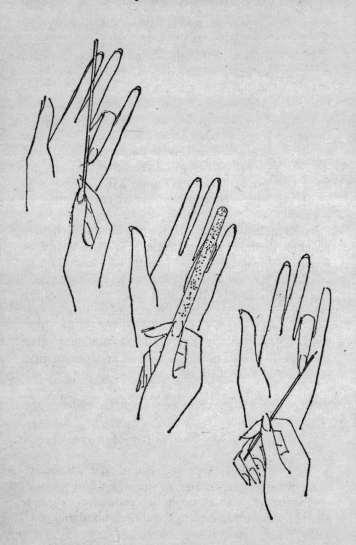

angewood stick, nail-polish remover, cuticle cream, pumice, cuticle scissors, base coat, nail polish, and top coat. Also a bowl of gently soaped water and one of clear water (for rinsing).

1. Remove any trace of old polish with a cotton ball that has been saturated with polish remover. Press the cotton firmly against the nail for a few seconds, then wipe with outward strokes. It may be necessary to repeat this step. Then dip a cotton-tipped swab stick into the remover and touch the sides and corners of the nails, as well as underneath, to be certain that all the old polish color is gone.

2. File your nails with the finest side of the new emery board, after first using the more abrasive side to trim and shape your nails down to the proper length you want (if they need shortening). If your nails have a tendency to break, then try to file them into a squared shape, with just an oval corner turn. They're less likely to break when the shape is squarish. File from sides toward the center, in one direction only, and always from underneath the nail.

3. Dip your fingertips into warm soapy water (you might add a cupful of baby oil) to clean your nails and to soften the cuticles. Then using the blunt end of a manicure stick wrapped in cotton, gently push the cuticles back. Never push at your cuticles with a metal or hard/sharp instrument; it can damage both the nail and cuticle. Now rinse the hand in clear water and dry gently with a clean towel.

4. Cover the cuticle area, the nail, and finger

with a conditioning cuticle cream and massage well, using a circular motion. This will stimulate the circulation and is good for the nails.

5. Avoid cutting your cuticles, which will only toughen the skin. Push back gently, and use cream daily if you tend toward dry skin. If you damage the base of the nail by cutting incessantly at the cuticle, you will eventually hinder the natural nail growth.

6. Use the pumice stone to gently rub any hardened skin formation, either at the edges of your fingertips or underneath.

7. Take a cotton swab stick, dip into some polish remover, and then clean well underneath each nail, making the tips as clean as you can.

8. Now, gently rinse your hand to make sure there is no dust or any kind of film from any of the lotions you have used.

9. Using a base-coat clear polish, run the brush over the top of the nail, to the underside. This will help nails from chipping. If your nails tend to break easily, you may want to use a special nail hardener in place of the base coat.

10. After the base coat has totally dried, apply your nail color. Use three strokes: first down the center of the nail, then down each side. This will help sweep up any streaks. After the first coat has dried (you'll be doing the other hand in between), then apply a second coat. Two coats will usually give a smooth finish.

11. After the nail polish has totally dried (allow at least ten minutes), apply a clear top or sealer coat over and remember to wrap this one around the nail tip as well.

12. Touch up the nail outline to make it free from smudges with a cotton swab dipped in the nail-polish remover. Then allow another ten minutes to assure that your nails are totally dry before using your hands.

How to Keep from Breaking Your Nails

As I have already explained, nails are very much like hair. They have some health problems—so that hair and nails can both be robbed of their luster and body strength. Nails don't have a direct blood supply and so good circulation can help nails to keep in shape.

Nails may also reflect any sickness you might be suffering from or medication that you are taking. Even if you're emotionally upset, the nails will reveal it, by breaking easily and becoming weak. Surprisingly, nails are thirsty for moisturizers—it's important to replenish the natural oils around the skin of the cuticles, so use a cream at least once daily.

Nails require constant protection—from soap and water, from abuses like dialing the phone or digging down into your handbag. First, always use rubber gloves when washing dishes or doing heavy housework. Next, learn to use the fingerpads and not your nails in typing, in dialing the phone, in any daily doings.

And believe it or not, nail polish will help nails in staying strong. So that even if you don't like bright colors, you can choose a soft pastel, or even a clear color, and apply daily to protect the nail.

What Will Stimulate Nail Growth?

Buffing with a good chamois buffer that you'll find at the dimestore or drugstore can stimulate the nail's circulation and help promote nail growth. Be sure to buff in one direction only, and not too fast, for the friction can cause too much heat and damage the nail surface. And of course, proper nutrition with enough protein is necessary as well for healthy nails.

What About Peeling Off Nail Polish?

This is a definite no-no. When you peel off the nail enamel, you're also peeling off the top protective coat of the nail. This will definitely weaken the nail and guarantee problems later on, like splitting and breaking. Use a polish remover—it's quick and it's easy. Some removers come in lemon and herbal scents, like Cutex; many have added conditioners to keep from drying out the nails.

Those Bubbles and Chips in Polish

If you have patiently given yourself a manicure and still find air bubbles forming that later chip and crack, that lead to an unsightly manicure, take heart. Bubbling nail enamel is almost always the result of not thoroughly cleaning your hands and nails before applying the polish. Oily residue, even those left from your fingertips touching the nails, can be the culprit. Be certain to wash and thoroughly dry your hands before applying polish.

That Thick Nail-Polish Problem

You can use a nail-polish thinner to try to salvage the thick nail polish you find in the bottle, or you might even try some paint thinner that you have around the house; it works in a similar manner. However, it is difficult to achieve the proper consistency with thinners. The best solution of all is a preventative one. Slow down the rate of thickening of your nail polish by keeping the bottle closed as much as possible and as often as you can. For instance, close it if you're interrupted in the middle of your manicure. And when you're all done, clean the neck of the bottle to ensure as tight a bottle-closing as possible.

The Professional Pedicure
You Can Do at Home

To do a perfect pedicure, you must treat your toes as carefully as you would your fingernails. Good foot care is every bit as necessary as good hand care. In fact, your feet get more usage and punishment and deserve pampering and attention. If you follow a regular pedicure plan and do it monthly, then you won't neglect

feet or toenails and you'll avoid any embarrassment
when you change from the boots of winter to the san-
dals of summer.

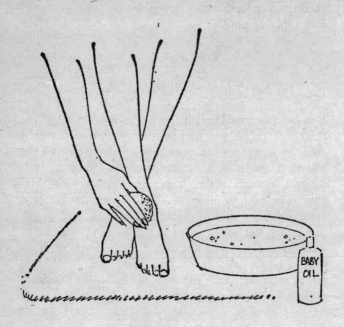

Footnotes

1. Prepare a big pot of foot soak, using soap,
water, and a quarter of a cup of baby oil. Toss in
some spearmint or peppermint leaves for an in-
vigorating treatment. Soaking your feet will
soften any calluses or corns and help you in using
a pumice stone most effectively in rubbing away
any dead or dry skin collections.

2. Soak your feet at least ten minutes each, using a pedicure brush to scrub any particularly hard or dry skin area.

3. Rub the ball and heel of each foot with a moderately coarse pumice stone, being careful not to rub too much in sensitive areas.

4. Trim the toenails straight across at the skin line with a large nail clipper. Then file down any catches left by the clipper. You'll want to leave your nails longer in sandal-baring weather. (Clip them shorter when you're wearing boots and hosiery most of the time.)

5. Now give yourself a mini-massage while you moisturize your legs and feet with a good cream. Start by kneading the arch of your foot with your fist. Continue to massage the upper part of your foot, where you rub the base of your toe, then massage up the calf of the leg.

6. Now twist a tissue and wind it in and out between your toes to hold them securely apart while you apply nail polish.

7. First put on a base coat, then follow with two coats of nail color, finally a top coat.

8. After each coat successfully dries (allow at least five minutes for each coat of polish), you can use a cotton swab and polish remover to remove any nail polish that might have smudged.

9. Follow up with some pleasant talcum or baby powder to keep your feet cool and fresh.

10. Toenails take beautifully to bright-colored polish, especially during summertime when you may be sporting a tan.

Product Cues

Dr. Scholl's has a complete line of foot-care products to help you help your feet. Everything from foot powder to foot balm to a pedicure brush to pumice stones will be found in most five and dime and discount stores that carry this total foot-care line. You'll also find lava stones that can be used to removed stubborn calluses, and some interesting foot soaks with which to treat your feet. Don't forget that Pond's creams and Mennen's Balm Barr Cocoa Butter Lotion are just two of the many good moisturizers on the market that you'll find can help with your foot-care problems.

Hand and Foot Therapy

After a hard day's work and walking on your feet—and using your hands for washing, typing, whatever work you do—you should treat them to some special care. All the beauty tips and products in the world won't work well if you're abusing your body. Relaxation, learning special techniques like acupressure point massage, can help you to help your body stay in tip-top shape. Here, some special points you can learn in giving both your hands and your feet a restful oriental type massage.

First:

- Bend the fingers of your left hand as if you are grasping something.

- Place your right thumb on the outside of the knuckle of the left index finger.
- Now, place the index finger of the right hand on the inside of the knuckle of the index finger of your left hand.
- Press for a slow count of ten, gently at first, then increasing the intensity on each count. Repeat three times on each hand.

Second:

- Run your thumb in a line between the big toe and second toe of your foot until you feel the large bone.
- Press thumb down just before the bone.
- Place the index finger on the sole of your foot underneath the thumb.
- Now, press fingers (as if together) for ten slow counts, gently at first and then increasing the pressure on each count. Repeat this accupressure therapy three times on each foot.

Third:

- Now, press the thumb on the fourth toe at the outside tip of the nail.
- Place your index finger on the spot just below the thumb on the sole of the toe.
- Gently press for ten slow counts, increasing the pressure on each count. Again, repeat three times on each foot.

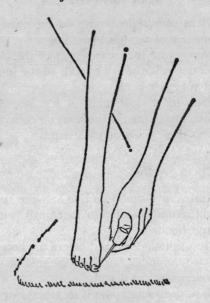

Final Reminders

Remember, the most important aspect of taking care of your hands and feet is first of all, keeping them soft and well manicured. Whether you invest in a professional manicure, or save money by doing it at home, the vital ingredient is time and patience. Unless each coat dries thoroughly, the next will be imperfect. Allow enough time, at least a half hour for a pedicure, and twenty minutes for a manicure, and give yourself another fifteen minutes after each before using your hands and feet. As with any aspect of beauty, a certain amount of effort has to be invested to achieve the desired results.

CHAPTER VI

Your Body

Self-Defense for Your Skin

The most important part of any skin-care program is proper cleansing, moisturizing, and protection from the elements. Your skin is a living, breathing cocoon. It's actually the single largest organ—spread out, it covers about fifteen thousand square inches. Put it on a scale and it weighs about six pounds. How you coax it, change it, cultivate it, is important. And you must always keep in mind that it isn't only your face that needs proper moisturizing and care—all of your body, from your head to your toes, elbows, knees, thighs, back—all of it deserves your attention.

The Aging Factor

We all have a built-in timer, but you can delay skin's aging with good habits. If we cut down on careless handling, which is responsible for the skin's irrational behavior after infancy, we would help protect our

skin. We wouldn't dare to touch our hearts, lungs, or any inner organs with the nonchalance most of us display toward the skin.

We now know from scientific studies that our wrinkles—and other age signs like skin discoloration and spots and sagging—are programmed genetically. Under a powerful microscope, the way the face is going to age can actually be seen on a baby's skin. How? In the form of lines that are invisible to the naked eye because of the subcutaneous fat layer that keeps them plumped out. These lines develop as you age, but their eventual visibility depends less on chronological time than on the way you live your life—specifically in the way you eat. Skin is also helped by exercise, which increases circulation by the extra intake of oxygen that is produced. Sleep and how much you get also affects your emotional life and your skin.

Becoming aware of good nutrition, of drinking at least eight glasses of water each day, of having enough fresh, leafy vegetables and fruits, enough protein, and cutting down or eliminating entirely alcohol, caffeine, and cigarettes, all of these will help you to maintain your skin's natural health. And of course, daily moisturizing and care will prevent harsh dryness and unsightly chafing, will help you to feel as soft and lovely as you can.

Just What Is a Moisturizer?

If you apply just one beauty rule to caring for your body, it should be to use a moisturizer. It should be used regardless of the hour, locale, season, or climate—even in summer when hot weather naturally produces more oil. The trick here is to switch to a lighter weight moisturizer, or if you have oily skin to begin with, to use a lighter weight one all year round. And of course, in the cold winter months, keeping your skin properly lubricated is even more important.

Most moisturizers serve in two ways. They hold your own natural moisture and add additional moisture through the emollients and water that constitute the ingredients of the product itself. Not only is some of the moisturizer absorbed by the skin, but a subtle film is also formed on the skin's surface and gives you protection. It's why you shouldn't towel dry after applying a moisturizer. It would defeat the purpose.

You might want to apply a good nourishing cream a few moments after you get into a steaming tub—the pores are open so the cream will penetrate very quickly and be absorbed. And of course, a loving massage with a body lotion after the shower or bath is vital. Apply the moisturizer when your body is still wet because it will penetrate better.

Silky, Gorgeous Skin All Over

The golden rule here: Always use a moisturizer all over your body at least once daily.

The preferred time: After your bath and shower. You can take a cream or lotion moisturizer and let your skin drink it all in. The pores are open right after a good steaming, and more of the product will be beneficial, and will be absorbed when your body is still wet.

Product Cues

You can use Johnson's Baby Oil or Baby Lotion or Lamston's or Woolworth's own brands of these same products, Nivea Moisturizing Lotion, Noxzema's Raintree Concentrated Moisture Maker for Extra Dry Skin, Pond's Dry Skin Cream, Lubriderm—or a host of other effective moisturizers that will help soften and moisturize your skin. Try them out in small sizes and find which product gives your body the best lubrication. In some cases you'll find that you want to use one on one day and then alternate to another.

Bathtub Exercises

Bathing has so many benefits. It relaxes while it cleanses; it gives you precious time away. If you will add a half cup of your favorite oil (baby oil or sesame or avocado) to the water, your body will get a soothing coating while you wash and cleanse.

There are lots of things you can do in the bathtub, but have you ever considered exercising? The water's buoyancy makes it quite effortless, compared, that is, to doing it on your hard, dry bedroom floor. Here are some basic routines to get you started. . . .

A. Semi-Situps. Keep legs together and straight, while sitting erect. Extend your arms, then bend from hips until your nose skims the water. Return to upright position. Repeat five times; work up to ten times if you can.

B. Leg and Arm Stretcher. Sit up straight, then place hands under buttocks with fingers turned in. Push up, keeping arms and legs straight, and lift body off bottom of tub at least a few inches. Relax back down. Repeat five times.

C. Thigh Exerciser. Lounge back in the bathtub and raise your arms over your head. Now, hold on to faucets or the rim of the tub. Raise one knee to your chest, keeping the other leg straight with your toe pointed. Hold for a second, then straighten the leg out. Now bend the other leg and bring the knee to the chest. Do ten times altogether, alternating each leg.

Sun Protection

Summer and suntans go together. Unfortunately so do the results of oversunning—painful burn, peeling, and the possiblity of long-term skin damage. It's those burning ultraviolet rays that do it. In the winter, too, in snow conditions, wherever you are unprotected out of doors during the highest sun hours of ten to four, a burn can be sustained. What to do? Never, but never, expose your body to the sun without a sunscreen product that contains a real sun block. Listed below, a representative sampling of some of the products you'll find on the market this year, available at the five and dime and discount stores.

Highest Protection
Block Out by Sea & Ski
Coppertone Super Shade by Plough
Bain De Soleil Super Block by Charles of the Ritz
PreSun by Westwood
Sun Bloc by Bonne Bell
Ultra Bloc by Bristol-Myers
Sundown by Johnson & Johnson
UVAL by Miles Labs

Moderate Protection
Sure Tan by Bonne Bell
Coppertone Shade by Plough
Bain De Soleil by Charles of the Ritz
Tropical Blend Butter and Spray by Plough

What to Do About Superfluous Hair

Historically, women have had different views of superfluous hair growth. In some societies hairy legs are in. In ours they're not, nor is a sudden sprouting on the chin or the upper lip. And yet hormonal changes will produce these superfluous hairs in almost all women at some time in their lives.

Smooth legs, underarms, and a hairless face is the preference of most American women. What are the best methods of dealing with each?

- For legs, you can resort to shaving, which is the most common although temporary method of hair removal. Or if you don't have an overabundant growth, then you might be satisfied with bleaching. This will disguise the soft downy hair and if you use a safe solution that isn't harmful to the skin, it should suffice.

- If you have embarrassing hair growth on the chin, the sides of your face, or on the upper lip, the only safe and permanent method of hair removal is electrolysis. It destroys the hair papilla with an electric current that feels like a tingle, and if you'll invest some time and money on this method, you'll achieve permanent hair-free results.

- As for tweezing, don't if it's an area that has superfluous hair. For tweezing actually stimulates coarser hair regrowth and eventually what may have started out as a minor problem will be a great big one.

Nature's Foods for Your Skin

Natural foods can make the best diets for the skin. And whether one is dealing with inner feeding—nutritional balance—or those organic items that you can feed the body topically, or externally, the fact remains that food taken in its natural state quite often has remedial powers.

In the last decade extensive evidence has been compiled indicating that a fatty, sugar-laden diet is a major factor in degenerative diseases and in premature aging. We all have heard of the damage that empty calories (white sugars and starches) and too much carbohydrate in the diet can do. From gastric upsets to diabetes, high blood-fat levels, hypoglycemia, heart disease, and atherosclerosis, the overconsumption of fatty foods and sugar-loaded ones is undeniably harmful to the system. Overeating is itself taxing to the organs, for the skin, don't forget, is an organ. Stretched skin, fat, layers of extra weight you don't need, are all the results of taking in too much food and too much of the wrong foods.

There are many foods that you can use for your skin, in recipes and remedies that come right from your kitchen. Let's take a look at some of those foods that can serve double duty.

- For blackheads. Slice a ripe tomato into 6 slices. Gently pack the affected area with the ripe slices, lie down; leave on five minutes, then rinse with 1/2 lemon to 1/2 cup water.
- For oily skin. First, wash your face with unsalted water in which cucumbers have been cooked. Then try this simple and effective mask: Beat the white of 1 egg with 1/2 teaspoon of honey and apply to face and neck liberally. Leave on for ten to fifteen minutes, then wash off with cold water—no soap. Egg white is the natural astringent and honey serves as the natural moisturizer. Together they can work mini-miracles on your skin.

- For oily skin. Applied several times during the day, lemon juice eliminates the sebum of oily skin. Used occasionally all over your body, it may clear up any discolorations, and soften and smooth. Even if it doesn't eliminate spots, it will restore a fresh feeling, and because it is acid it can help restore the body's natural acid mantle.

- For hand care. Coat your hands with a mixture of equal parts fresh lemon juice, glycerine, and a drop of your favorite eau de cologne.

- For brittle nails. Apply fresh-squeezed lemon juice from a half a lemon directly on your nails, morning and evening, for at least one week. If it works, continue. If not, try adding an egg yolk to the lemon by mixing in a cup and then soak hands in this mixture, bathing the nail area.

- To brighten teeth. Use the rind of a lemon with a bit of the pulp and rub back and forth daily. Tip: If soaked in hot water for five minutes before being cut and squeezed, lemons will yield more juice.

- For an all-over body treatment. Applied directly to the skin, finely grated carrots can facilitate the development of fresh cells. Rub gently, massaging each area as you use the carroty paste.

- For sallow skin or chafed areas. Use the juice of 2 carrots mixed with 2 tablespoons of plain yogurt and allow to remain on for ten minutes. Rinse with lemon and water mixture.

- For an all-over body sloughing. The papaya fruit can do wonders. Toss into your blender

with a half a lemon and then apply as a paste
to all parts of your body. One papaya should
do it. Allow to remain on at least fifteen minutes. Then rinse off under a tepid shower.

● For soothing irritated or chafed skin due to
abrasion or hypersensitivity. Mix 1/4 cup of
honey to 1 egg yolk and 4 tablespoons of yeast
powder. Pierce 1 400-unit vitamin E capsule
with a sterilized needle and add in the oil to
the rest of the ingredients. Mix well and apply
as a salve to any dry or lined or irritated area
of the skin. Allow to remain on at least fifteen
minutes. Rinse gently with lukewarm water.

An Oatmeal Bath

Want a low-cost treatment that will bring relief to dry
skin, help dermatitis, eczema, or any other similar skin
disorder? Try oatmeal in a bath.

Just dissolve an envelope of instant oatmeal in 3/4
cup of hot milk and form a paste. Tie this oatmeal
paste into a smooth cloth, perhaps an old handker-
chief or a doubled piece of cheesecloth. Then use it
like a big soap bar in a lukewarm bath, rubbing the
paste gently all over your body, and especially in those
dry, scaly areas. The liquid will ooze through the paste
and soothe as it cleanses.

De-Winterizing Your Skin

One quick method to add an appealing oily glow from head to toe and get rid of all those dried-out, arid spots: Mash up a ripe avocado, smear it from head to toe right after your bath, and then lie back and give yourself twenty minutes of natural relaxation and moisturizing. After that, if you still find an area that needs further softening, spread room-temperature mayonnaise carefully on the damaged area. Finally, a good shower and a rubdown with a Loofa sponge which you can find in a health-food store, will stimulate circulation and remove any scaly patches and old skin. Finish up with an all-over moisturizer that will give your skin a smooth and silky look.

(By the way, oily skin can be dehydrated too and need the same treatment.)

CHAPTER VII

For Those Special People and Situations

FOR TEEN-AGERS

Squeaky Clean Beginnings

Cleanliness is next to freshness. Believe in being clean. Make it a habit. The teen years can be self-conscious ones as you go through the normal growing pains. It takes time to get used to it all. Being comfortable with others begins with being comfortable with yourself, and this implies head-to-toe freshness and neatness and taking care of the basics, taking care of you.

To be fresh means there is no trace of perspiration odor. Beginning with adolescence on up, practically everyone perspires. In fact two to three quarts of liquid are lost each day due to perspiration. If you're under emotional, physical, or nervous stress, then a lot more is lost. It's nice to know that perspiration itself is odorless; however, if it remains on the skin, certain bacteria disintegrate and begin to create those undesirable odors.

Not to worry. If you'll shower or bathe with water

and soap daily, the washing will help your body remain free of bacteria, the basic cause of body odor. To get the most out of your daily cleansing, every area of the body should have individual attention. The creases and folds of the skin need special care, since perspiration and flying dust build up in these parts. The armpits, genital and anal sections, the toes, and the parts in front of and behind the ears should be washed daily.

If you have very dry skin you might follow up a shower with a soothing body cream like Johnson's Baby Cream or Baby Lotion. You might also add one quarter of a cup of Johnson's Baby Oil into the bathwater to help make your skin feel smooth and softer.

If you have no special skin problems, it's advisable to use softened water when taking a bath. In hard water the soap may create a feeling of dryness, or worse, an itchiness. You might use bath salts that act as water softeners. Unless your doctor advises, it's not necessary to use medicated soaps.

Après Bath Protection

You'll help protect your body from the elements—wind, water, sun, and bitter cold—by using a protective layer of a soothing oil. Anything from simple petroleum jelly to Pond's cream to Johnson's Baby Cream to Elizabeth Post Moisture Cream can help. After sunning, Johnson's Baby Oil can take away any dry or itchy feeling and help hide any peeling or flaking.

Walk, Don't Run

Gentleness and purity are the prime ingredients in good body care. Starting habits early will help you form good ones and keep to them. Diet, exercise, getting enough sleep, are all vital factors in how you look and feel. So pay attention to your body and move it regularly to keep that healthy glow. A daily mile stroll, fast walking, jogging, are just some of the easiest forms of exercise you might try on for size. They need little or no special equipment and can be done almost anywhere in any kind of weather. The most important step of all is to try to introduce and then follow a regular, daily program. Remember, good habits can be learned just as well as bad.

The amount of sleep required varies from person to person, usually between six and nine hours. By the way you feel, you will know what is adequate for you. Once you do, adjust your schedule to assure yourself of getting a continuous good night's rest.

Tension is the villain of both body and mind. It is difficult to avoid in this competitive busy world, we know. However, it is quite possible to learn how to relax, how to communicate with others to avoid misunderstandings, and how to see the world as a positive environment and you a positive part of it. Be creative and discover your own ways of letting go. If you feel unhappy and depressed and it has been lasting a long while, then discuss it with your religious counselor or school counselor and seek outside help in learning how to cope. Get up and get out and make the changes that will make your life work.

Hair Is Your Crowning Glory

Hair in the now is shining and clean, carefree, and natural. Easy looks are best for teen-agers, and a good hairstyle begins with a proper shaping and cut. Here it pays to invest in a professional cutting that will set the line and help you maintain your hair easily. A regular program of grooming to keep your hair in lustrous shape and an efficient shampooing and conditioning regimen are all part of your beauty plan.

Insist on a cut that harmonizes with your facial

structure, height, and hair characteristics, and one that can be worn in more than one way. Even with the best of cuts, however, your hair won't look as good as it can if it isn't in good condition. Split hair ends from over blow-drying or bleaching might become a problem. Avoid it by starting early to learn the proper way to care for your hair.

Protect your hair from the torrid sun as well as the cold elements. Wear a scarf or a hat, as well as headbands and tied-back hairdos when out of doors. Of course, any headcovering should be free enough to prevent perspiration from accumulating, and the hair from being unnecessarily pulled.

Rinse saltwater and chlorine out of your hair as soon as possible after a swim; they are both potentially harmful to your hair.

Wet hair should be treated gently. In this form hair is at its most vulnerable and is subject to breakage. Gently towel-dry, slowly work tangles out with a wide-toothed comb, and never brush in the wet stage. Curlers that are wound too tightly are also a no-no. It's best to gently dry the hair on a cool setting on the hair dryer, or with a towel, then brush and gently set if you need some curl.

Be sure to use the correct implements. Brushes with jagged edges, sharp-toothed combs with teeth missing, are only going to break, scratch, or pull out your hair.

For Dry Hair

Shampoo only as often as needed with a gentle conditioning product, such as Bonne Bell Good Nature

Shampoo or Johnson's Baby Shampoo. Both are gentle and can be used safely on dry hair. Of course, a good conditioning with egg and oil, at least once weekly, will help to restore the necessary texture and oils that are missing. One easy recipe: Use one egg yolk to a half cup of avocado, apricot, or olive oil; mix well and apply to dry hair. Allow to remain on at least a half hour, working it through. Then rinse well, using a mild shampoo.

There are also many commercial conditioning products that you can purchase at the dimestore and discount store—everything from Wella Kolestral to Bonne Bell Honest Hair Conditioner to Nestle and Breck products—you'll find a wealth of rinses and conditioners to add to your thirsty hair.

Of course, if you live in an area where you have dry heat conditions in the winter, a humidifier is the best protection of all. It can help your hair and skin be shielded from the effects of steam heat. If you can't afford a humidifier, a pot of water on the radiator helps.

For Oily Hair

Keep your scalp and hair as clean as you can. Skin breakouts, dandruff, and even scalp conditions can be caused by an excess of oil and bacteria that collect on oily hair. A shampoo made specifically for oily hair, like gentle pH-balanced Ten-O-Six shampoo by Bonne Bell, or even a dandruff-fighting shampoo like Head & Shoulders, will help stave off quick oil collection.

Rinsing with vinegar, a half a cup to a cup of water, will also aid in combating oiliness.

Avoid overbrushing your hair. Ironically, this stimulates the scalp and can increase the oiliness. And when you do brush your hair, avoid the scalp area.

Always rinse your hair with cool to cold water. Too much heat activates the oil on your scalp. In the same manner, when you use your blow-dryer, avoid the very hot setting, which will actually stimulate the oiliness too. And in a pinch, when you can't wash your hair and want to look your freshest, you can take some talcum powder, put it on a brush, and brush through your hair. The dust and dirt will cling to the brush in this manner. You can also take a nylon stocking, wrap it around a hairbrush, apply a bit of cornstarch or talcum powder, and brush through your hair well. Again, the powder will absorb some of the oiliness.

End Split Ends

No, you don't have to go through life with split ends. Starting now to form good habits will help keep your hair at its healthiest. First, trim hair regularly. Splits will journey up the hair shaft, so it's very important to keep them from spreading. Second, avoid using the blow-dryer on a daily basis. And if you must wash and blow-dry daily, then let your hair air-dry most of the way and then use the dryer only for the final fullness, always on a warm and not hot setting.

Conditioning your hair after each shampoo will help. Adding an egg yolk to the shampoo monthly will also give your hair nourishment. And a good application, also at least once a month, of a pack made with a half cup of mayonnaise can also do wonders. Johnson's Baby Oil, Bonne Bell Honest Hair Conditioner, Fabergé conditioning shampoo—all of these products that you can find at your local discount or chain or dimestore will also be beneficial.

Skin Deep

Clear, soft, unblemished skin is every woman's desire. It is within the grasp of most teens, unless you have a special acne condition. In this case you'll have to work harder, and know what is good and what isn't for your particular skin, and what priority products and habits you should form.

The skin is always producing cells. They form in the deepest layers, make their way to the surface, and are finally sloughed off, or shed. Skin cells produce "sebum," a natural oil that helps keep your skin smooth and retain moisture. To help stave off infection, your skin also needs to maintain a natural acid balance, which is called a pH of about 4.5 to 6.5. This represents the natural mantle of acid that forms upon the skin.

Normal Skin

Normal is an odd term, we know, for what is normal to one person is far from normal to another, and genes and heredity certainly play a part in what we must work with. Still, you will recognize your skin as being within the normal zone if it doesn't break out excessively, if it isn't too oily or too dry, and you have small pores and a good tone to your complexion. Following a regular schedule then of cleansing and moisturizing it day and evening will keep it as normal as it should be. There are a host of wonderful creams and soaps that you may use from your teens right on, and they don't cost a fortune. Here is a list of just some of those products that can do the job:

Soaps and Moisturizers

Johnson's Baby Soap

Alpha Keri Soap

Neutrogena Dry-Skin Soap or Baby Soap

Dove

Nivea Creme Soap

Happy Face Facial Washing Cream

Johnson's Baby Oil Cleanser

Pond's Cold Cream

Noxzema Skin Cream

Noxzema Raintree Moisture Maker

Nivea Creme

Toni Deep Magic Moisturizer Cream

Jergens Wash Tub Lathering Face Wash

Bonne Bell Sport Lotion

Bonne Bell Body Soak Moisturizing

Bath/Shower Gelee

Bonne Bell Ten-O-Six Cleansing Bar

Johnson's Baby Cream

Dry Skin

Most teen-agers don't have dry skin. Young skin sheds old cells easily; however, as we age the skin sometimes needs assistance. If those old cells are not regularly shed, they can build up and appear leathery and coarse. So do be prepared. The elements can cause areas of dryness—so that if you're out skiing or sunning you may find chafed, rough parts on your body. Wind, water, sun, heat, even air conditioning are contributing factors that are continually stealing the moisture from skin by evaporation.

If you tend to have dry skin, take special measures. For instance, if you find rough patches on your elbows and knees, you may need to reinforce these areas by putting a half cup of oil in your bathwater daily, then using an oatmeal paste (1/2 cup of rough-cut oatmeal to 1/4 cup of water) and rubbing this gently over the rough parts of your skin. Follow up always with a good moisturizing cream.

Cleaning your skin daily will help remove old, dead cells, the main cause of those dry and flaky areas. You might want to investigate using one of the buff puffs on some of the less sensitive areas, or purchase a Loofa, a dry natural sponge that you can use to soap yourself up with during your shower or bath. These implements can help remove cells that are flaky, and stimulate your circulation as well. Some of the products you might use that are excellent for dry-skin types are:

Soaps and Moisturizers
Nivea Creme Soap

Aveenobar
Dove
Pond's Creamy Facial Cleanser
Pond's Dry Skin Cream
Lubriderm Moisturizer
Noxzema's Raintree Concentrated
Moisture Maker for Extra Dry Skin
Johnson's Baby Oil
Johnson's Baby Lotion

Oily Skin

If your skin's glands are producing more than enough
sebum, then clogged pores will result. The result can
often be an embarrassing breakout of blackheads,
whiteheads, and blemishes. The most effective treatment for oily skin is proper cleansing. This doesn't
mean that you should reach for the strongest cleanser
you can find. Harsh soaps and astringents can create
more problems by triggering the oil glands and upset-
ting the skin's natural acid-mantle balance. If you use
a harsh product with alcohol in it, it will actually
stimulate oil and create more problems than it will
help.

Instead, get into the habit of cleansing your skin
with pH-balanced products, which you'll find clearly
stated on the label. For instance, Ten-O-Six by Bonne
Bell falls within the pH-adjusted category. It is also
available in a cleansing bar, a deep-pore technique
that fights bacteria, helps heal blemishes, and removes
extra oiliness. Noxzema is an excellent cleanser also,

just add a bit of water and wash the face with this creamy, medicated cream.

Besides a regular cleansing schedule, a good washing with grains can help slough off dead skin cells and sweep away some of the impurities from the skin's surface. A good home grain can be made with either cornmeal or oatmeal, both cereal products you'll find in the kitchen, or at the supermarket. Merely take 1/4 cup of either rough-cut oatmeal or cornmeal, mix with just enough milk to form a good paste, and then gently rub on your face, avoiding the delicate areas around the eyes and above the lips. This will help to stimulate the circulation, as well as serve as an abrasive type exfoliating product.

By the way, oily skin can be toned down with a lemon rinse. Here, take a half a lemon, squeeze well, mix with 1/4 cup of lukewarm water, then gently sponge on your face, or use a cotton ball to gently wash your face in this mildly acid solution. It's a good idea to use the lemon rinse at least once daily, either after removing your makeup at the end of the day, or before applying your makeup in the morning, after you have washed your face in your regular manner.

Bonne Bell also has Ten-O-Six Cleansing Tissues that you can tuck into your purse to use in the middle of the day for touch-ups of oil-blotting. Andrea Fresh-Ups, facial linen blotters, are another product you will find in the discount and chain store that can help blot up the extra oil that may form during your busy day.

Combination Skin

Most of us have combination skins—oily in some parts, dry in others. In this case it's a good idea to follow the rules of caring for each that you'll find in the oily or dry instructions. Of course, you won't use moisturizer on very oily sections, nor would you scrub and rub with beauty grains those areas that are delicate and dry. Common sense is an important ingredient to any beauty program. If you're not sure, ask. Your skin is a reflection of you and how you care for it.

Let's Face It

Smoking encourages wrinkles, the pouty lines about the mouth, and a yellowing of the skin as you age. It also affects the circulation of the body, and circulation is what keeps skin in the best of tone and tenacity. So if you haven't already formed this bad habit, don't. And if you have, you can stop now, before it gets to be a major addiction. Smoking is no longer a glamorous in-thing to do, so don't. If you can't stop smoking on your own, attend a free stop smoking clinic given by The American Cancer Society. Look up the chapter near you in your telephone directory.

And now is the time also to avoid forming other bad habits for your face. Like leaning on it with your hands, which can create sagging chin muscles and other problems later. Also removing your makeup at the end of the day is a must—you need only five minutes before bedtime to do a proper job—for laziness is a no-no here.

Teen-age Dilemma

Teen skin problems often last a few years, and in some cases can be prevented. Here are some of the rules to avoid skin problems where you can:

- Wash your face at least once daily.
- Avoid highly perfumed soaps and alcohol-containing products.
- Keep hair clean by shampooing frequently.
- Use fresh towels and washcloths.
- Change pillowcases frequently.

What About Acne?

Acne is a very common condition which most people—both men and women—have in some degree during their adolescent or early adult years. No two individuals will experience the same condition of acne. It may range all the way from a few scattered blackheads to a severe, infected, scarring eruption in another situation. In each case there are different causes and treatments, and so it would be well for you to see a doctor, preferably a specialist in skin problems, a dermatologist.

There are many medicated skin lotions you may use

after first consulting with the doctor. From Medicated Acne Defense by Bonne Bell to Noxzema to Clearasil ointment and soaps, you'll find a host of temporary helpers in the dimestores and discount stores.

There is no single cause for the common eruption known as acne, but rather many different factors have varying importance in each case. Some of them are:

- Hormonal influences. Certain chemicals or hormones are produced in the adrenal glands and reproductive organs. During teen years these hormonal substances act on overly susceptible sebaceous glands, resulting in whiteheads, blackheads, and oiliness, the distinctive signs of acne.
- Local infection. A papule, pustule or infected cyst all represent the effects of bacterial infection in plugged sebaceous glands.
- Dietary factors. The role of certain foods in causing skin outbreaks remains a controversial question. In some cases particular foods, oily and fatty ones, can aggravate the disease of acne; in others there doesn't seem to be a clear relationship. However, drinking lots of water, avoiding fats and fried foods, iodine-containing foods like shrimp, and keeping away from sweets usually will help.

Facing the World Prettily

Makeup can add a glow to your already glowing face. Unless you have a very poor skin condition, and must avoid clogging of the pores, makeup can make you feel even better about yourself. A satisfactory daytime application may include a bit of foundation, some eye shadow, rouge, mascara, and lip color or gloss. Makeup for the evening would be the same, but you would use more so that it will still show up in the artificial lighting. Match your face to suit your mood, where you are going, and your own personal life-style. Makeup, properly applied, can enhance. Improperly used, it will make you look harsh, older, and cheap. So if you're intending to use makeup, now is the time to learn how to use it well.

Foundation

The use of a makeup base is to smooth out the tone and texture of your skin, and not to add color. Select the shade nearest to your own skin tone by testing it on your jawline. The right shade will look most natural when you compare it with your throat area. Don't hestitate to mix your foundation tones to form your own particular color—this type of blending often creates the most natural results.

First, apply the foundation over your entire face, even the eye area. Be sure it's well blended. You might dab it all over with a slightly damp sponge, or after applying with your fingertips, gently smooth in upward strokes.

If your face is flat or wide, you can also use foundation to contour. Here you'll select a shade that is about three shades darker than your own skin tone, and use it to shadow and contour those areas that you want to diminish in width or largeness. For instance, suck in your cheeks and apply the deeper foundation to that area of the cheek you want to dramatize— because it will give you a gaunt Katharine Hepburn look if you use a darker shade. Similarly, you'll highlight those areas, that you want to stand out with either a pink-colored pencil or a lighter shade of foundation. For instance, here you might want to play up your center part of your nose if it is straight. Also if you want to narrow a too-wide nose, apply a lighter foundation straight down the center. (For in-depth contouring instructions, see Chapter IV, Contouring.)

For concealing under-eye shadows and circles, you can use a concealing cream like Bonne Bell Cover Cream or White White. Try various eye-shadow colors and combinations too, for concealing value. Light shades bring the eyes forward, darker shades help them recede. FlameGlo Soft-Eyes pencil shadow can do the trick too. Colláge has an eye-shadow collection that also offers light-medium-dark tones that you can use for contouring.

Product Cues

Maybelline Oil-Control Make-Up
Natural Wonder Fresh-All-Day Oil-Blotting Makeup
Bonne Bell Medicated Make-Up
Colláge Moisture Base Make-Up
Maxi Moist Make-Up
Cover Girl Liquid Make-Up
Ultra Sheen Liquid Make-Up
Maybelline Moisture Whip Cream Make-Up

Eye Lights

Even if you choose not to wear makeup base, you'll want to play up your pretty eyes. The correct application of eye makeup can give you almost any emphasis you'd like, for your eyes are your most expressive feature. Remember, the main focus should be on your eyes, and not on the makeup. Smudge or blend the colors to soften any harsh edges and to create a natural look. Nothing dates one faster than how one's eyes are made up. You can go to those old movies and tell that a woman was a teen-ager in the 1930's by her eyebrows and eye shadow; and you can tell the woman who grew up in the 1950's by her using exaggerated eyelashes or extending her eyeliner in Cleopatra fashion. You're a teen, growing up in the eighties, a time for natural makeup looks. Work with them now, and change as the years go by, so you'll always look your prettiest and freshest.

Mascara is all important. Even when you don't want to dress your eyes with eye shadow, do use a bit of mascara. From Maybelline to Noxzema to Cover Girl to FlameGlo you'll find a wealth of mascaras in cake, cream, wand, and roll-on forms, in just as many shades, all at a variety store.

To remove eye makeup, White Rose Makeup Remover Petroleum Jelly is handy, as is Johnson's Baby Oil. Andrea also makes Eye Q's eye makeup remover pads that removes even waterproof mascara efficiently. It's available in a thirty-five- or eighty-pad jar.

Beauty and the Blush

Select a blush formula that goes best with your skin type. Oilier skins are more compatible with a powder blush, while if your skin is dry, you'll probably find a cream blush more satisfactory. Experiment—most products offer samples and you can always go to your local department store and try on every type of product that you can then duplicate in the dimestore or discount store.

To apply blush, you'll need to find the triangle that is formed by the top of your ear, the tip of your earlobe, and the inside corner of your cheekbone. For a healthy glow you might also apply a bit of the blush to your chin and forehead area. Do it all naturally, of course, and avoid using too much color during the day.

Makeup for Sports Activities

Try an active look with the focus on fresh and natural color in a face gloss or bronzer. Then use a sheer gloss for really shiny lips. You'll find FlameGlo, Maybelline, and Bonne Bell all with a host of makeup colors that work here.

Use pinks, peaches, and tawny shades like a deep copper or bronze on your cheeks to create a really radiant look. Avoid eye shadow, or if your lids require color, use a tawny taupe or cocoa, something that is natural and won't stand out. Then apply lots of mascara in brown, deep brown, or black, depending on your coloring. Freshen lips with lip gloss or one of those super lip applications by Bonne Bell or Maybelline that come in flavors. They're fun. Wear cool, clean cologne scents like Jean Naté or 8020 Cologne, or even one of those natural oils, lavender or gardenia, that you'll find sold in health-food shops, as a sporty accessory, and make sure that if you're going to be in the sun, you don't apply the cologne or oils to the skin, as it can discolor during a tanning. Of course, always use sun-block products to assure you're not drying out the skin during sun exposure.

Makeup for Evening Dates

Switch for the evening to a focus on deeper colors. Perhaps sultry wines, or ravishing plums, rich raisins; each intense shade can give you that glamorous look. Always use shades that are harmonious with your skin tone and eye color. A deep wine lipstick, for instance, on someone with very fair skin may give a gaudy look—always go just one shade darker. Never wear rouge or lipstick that is obviously dark on you or you'll look like you're making up to haunt a house. Try red, burgundy, or rose to highlight your cheeks. A trick: Add a bit of gold-colored eye shadow, made by Maybelline and Max Factor, to the center apple of your cheek for a spicy highlighter in the evening.

For eyes try gray or a navy blue as a dazzling starlight look. Using deep brown or black or even navy mascara can add to the effect. For your lips a purple

or wine gloss over your regular color will add a unique
look. Match your fingertips in a polish that is burgundy or wine for dress-up occasions. Warm, earthy
scents of cologne can complement your evening look.

Makeup that Lasts All Day

A light dusting of translucent face powder will help to
hold your foundation, eye shadow, and blush. Carry
some along for later dusting. An empty spice container
with perforated top, or an old pill container, can hold
the loose powder securely in your purse.

There are also many good pressed powders that
come in their own compacts that are wonderful for
quick touch-ups. Pond's and Angel Face and Cover
Girl all have pressed powders in natural and translucent shades.

Buzz Words

Here are some general tips just for teens that can help
you on your path to beauty:

- The normal hair-growth rate is about one half
  inch per month. Hair grows most between the
  ages of sixteen and twenty-four, and a woman's
  hair rarely grows longer than three feet. Good
  conditioning, regular cleansing, and proper
  trimming are good habits to form early.
- Never go to sleep with your makeup on.

Clogged pores, unsightly pillowcase stains, and not giving your skin an opportunity to breathe will be the bad result. A few extra moments at day's end is well worth the time.

- For most individuals a shower or bath alone won't keep away perspiration or its odor. Underarm deodorant and/or an antiperspirant usually are necessary. From Ban to Arrid to Jean Naté to Mitchum, you'll find a host of products at your drugstore and discount store. A deodorant neutralizes odor, and an antiperspirant decreases perspiration after application. You might also try dress shields if you find you are going through a period where you are staining your clothes.

- You can shave your legs using a bit of Johnson's Baby Lotion, which enables your razor to slide along effortlessly and will reduce the chance of nicks and cuts.

- If you suffer from rough, red hands, try putting a pair of loose-fitting white cotton gloves over them after you have applied a coating of petroleum jelly. You might use your hair dryer to create warmth, or, better still, keep the gloves on all night while you sleep.

- For teen-age acne, medicated astringent types of foundations are the best for cover-ups.

- A soft metallic or pearl shadow on the eyelids can give you a terrific evening look. In lipsticks stay with the clear, fresh colors and avoid very blue colors like fuchsia, which can look too old or tinselly, on young faces.

- Never use your fingernails or fingertips to remove a blackhead or whitehead. If you can't do it with sterile cotton and witch hazel, see your dermatologist, who can teach you a proper cleansing procedure.

FOR THE PREGNANT WOMAN

The Doctor's View

"Pregnancy is not a disease and shouldn't be treated as one. There's no need for a normal pregnant woman to isolate herself for forty weeks," says prominent gynecologist/obstetrician, Alois Vasicka, who has been Chief of Obstetrics and Gynecology at a hospital in New York and is now affiliated with the Albert Einstein School of Medicine in Manhattan. Dr. Vasicka advises that "a woman must be in command of her pregnancy. She should run it and not let it run her." And so after you have seen your doctor and as long as he tells you your pregnancy is a normal one, then continuing to maintain the moderate exercise programs you did before, and treating yourself to the cosmetic niceties you enjoy using—all of these options are yours. As long as you stay away from harsh chemicals, read the ingredients on the labels carefully, and ask if you're not sure what any medication contains, taken orally or topically, you'll be okay.

Pregnancy brings a whole new set of beauty situations, from changes in skin and hair to your body. Simplicity, naturalness, and a new awareness on just what is and isn't good for you during the term of childbearing, are all important factors in your beauty plan.

First, you should adjust to the fact that changes are going to take place. If this is your first baby, it may mean that you should read some good books on the subject, share with other mothers-to-be and consult with your doctor. After all, you want to experience the best and most beautiful pregnancy you can. Knowledge and awareness will help you cope with changes as they come up.

Hormones are the major reason that you'll find incredible changes taking place in your skin, hair, and shape. Even your senses will go through a metamorphosis, so that certain tastes, smells, and feelings will be different. Not to worry. It's all part of human nature and motherhood.

Skin Care

During the first three months you may experience dry skin because of an increase in estrogen. If your skin feels drier than usual, and you notice little dry patches and areas of sensitivity, use a moisturizer as often as you can. Gentle soap and water washes, followed by constant nourishment with creams, will help. Avoid any ointments or creams—like Lydia O'Leary and Eterna 27, to name just a couple—that contain hormones or bleaches. If you're not sure if the ingredients are safe during pregnancy, ask your doctor. The skin does absorb what you put on it.

If your skin becomes oily, which is caused by an in-

crease in another hormone, progesterone, then you
may have to deal with sudden breakouts and blemishes, as well as clogged and enlarged pores. In this
case a good cleansing at least twice a day will help,
followed by a sponging with witch hazel, which is a
safe astringent. Then apply moisturizer around the
delicate areas, like the throat and around your eyes.
And if the oiliness gets so bad that you develop acne,
try pHisoDerm or Cuticura soaps. See your dermatologist if it gets so bad you can't control it.

Product Cues

Just as for baby, you can always use Johnson's Baby
Soap for cleansing your skin during pregnancy. Consider also Johnson's Baby Oil and Lotion. And many
variety stores have their own bargain brand versions of
the oil, soap and lotion, so do look for these products,
which give you the same results even more cheaply.
If you have ultra dry skin, Neutrogena's dry-skin soap
and Nivea Skin Oil can help. And don't forget, there
are many natural recipes and remedies you'll find
throughout this book that you can also use safely.

The Pregnancy Mask

It happens to many women, this unique pigmentation
change that is due to an overstimulation of the hormone MSH. The result: a sort of mask pattern across
the nose and cheeks in brownish spots. Although it

might be unsightly when it occurs, just a bit of makeup foundation can cover it, and it will fade soon after delivery. However, be certain to use an effective sun block if you will be sunning, for the sun will increase the pigmentation and you'll find it takes a great deal longer to get rid of it. Some makeups contain a sunscreen in them, like Maybelline's Moisture Whip and Face Quencher by Chap Stick. You'll find them in a range of shades at your local dimestore and discount store.

Facial Masks

You need time to relax and think positive thoughts. You'll also look better if you'll develop the habit of giving yourself a weekly facial mask. This will be beneficial to every skin type, including dry and oily skin, for a gentle mask is natural, it stimulates the circulation, and acts as a deep cleanser. Following are two excellent facial mask recipes, both natural and nourishing and meant to baby you.

STRAWBERRY-YOGURT MASK: Take 2 tablespoons plain yogurt, add 2 tablespoons fresh strained strawberry juice (you can use frozen strawberries if fresh ones aren't in season) and stir by hand until smooth. Add 1 egg white and beat to a stiffer consistency. Then apply to your face, lie back, put cotton pads that have been cooled in the refrigerator on your eyelids, and think beautiful thoughts about motherhood for at least twenty minutes. There you have it, a creamy, good-for-your-skin face mask that costs pennies. Rinse off with room temperature mineral water with the juice of half a lemon added for pH balance.

PEACHES AND CREAM MASK: Remove the pits and cut up 2 really ripe peaches. Toss pieces into blender with 1/8 cup heavy cream or 1/8 cup buttermilk. If you don't have a blender, you can mash and whip by hand. Get the ingredients to a smooth consistency, then lie down, feet up, and cover your face and neck with this delicious mask. Let set for at least fifteen minutes, then rinse off with cool water in a circular motion.

On Your Hair

Hormones here too can affect how you look, for you may experience some hair loss during pregnancy and even after. Be assured it will grow back, that it may even be stronger and more luxurious later. However, you should take special precautions during this time to treat your hair gently. For instance, be certain of what products you use. Shampoos are chemicals, believe it or not. So are permanents, which can present a special problem during pregnancy, and in many individuals perms don't take well. Check ingredients, use safe and as many natural cosmetics and hair-care products as you can, and when in doubt check with your doctor. Even simple implements like brushes can make a difference to your hair. Be sure to use a soft, natural bristle hairbrush which will not stretch or pull or break the hair.

Hair rollers can still be used, but avoid any hot settings on rollers or with dryers. And limit use as much as possible. You can towel-dry your hair and then use the blower to finish off the job.

Hair conditioning is very important during this time. Here are two totally natural hair conditioners you can use that are safe and, best of all, cheap.

FOR HAIR BREAKAGE TREATMENT: Shampoo your hair with a gentle pH-balanced shampoo, or a mild one like Johnson's Baby Shampoo. Then cover your entire scalp and hair with a mixture of 1/4 cup mayonnaise, 1/8 cup blackstrap molasses, and 1/8 cup soy sauce. Wrap your head in plastic and leave it on for at least twenty minutes. Rinse well, then shampoo once again with a gentle shampoo. This treatment, if done weekly, will help restore brittle ends and smooth any splits to give a softer appearance.

FOR TREATING OILY HAIR: Sometimes during pregnancy you go through a very oily skin and hair period. To rid the hair of those oily strains, get a box of dry oat flakes, use 1/2 cup for long hair, a little less for short hair, and slowly and firmly work the dry flakes into your oily hair. Now, get a brush and start brushing those oil-absorbed flakes out. Brush and then brush some more, stimulating the scalp as you do. It will do wonders for the oil, blotting most of it up, and will give your hair a gentle but needed brushing.

After using the brush, it's time to do a good shampooing. Here, choose one of the shampoos like Ogilvie or Breck for oily hair. You'll find a vast assortment of others, too, in the discount stores. In this case purchase smaller sizes, even though they aren't as economical. Hair seems to tire of the same product, and if you'll give it variety, by using one brand and alternating with another, you will get better results. Finally, after rinsing at least twice to rid your hair of any oatmeal residue, rinse with a solution of 1/3 cup water to 2/3 cup apple cider vinegar. Rinse once again. And again.

Special Hand Care

If you find your hands looking a bit less lovely than usual, then you may need some special moisturizing treatments. Of course, continue with pretty manicures and pedicures that will make you feel good about yourself. You'll find all the steps to give yourself home applications in Chapter V. Here are tips for special handling of your hands:

1. The first rule is moisturizing. A good moisture-replenisher that imparts an improved tone and texture to your skin is important. Treat your hands to a good skin softening lotion. (Pond's Cream & Cocoa Butter Skin Softening Lotion and Johnson's Baby Cream are two products that are popularly priced and effective.)

2. Keep bottles of lotion conveniently located throughout your home—in the bedroom, bathroom, and kitchen. Make sure that you have a purse-size (refillable) bottle whenever you go out. Your hands will never have to go without a "drink" of rich moisture.

3. Always use lotion after your hands come in contact with water and before you go to bed.

4. Let housework work for you, by giving your

hands a generous luxurious treat. Before you start
your chores, apply an ample slathering of lotion
to your hands. Put on a pair of cotton gloves, then
a pair of rubber household gloves. Now go about
your work. When you remove both pairs of gloves
you'll find that your hands will be smooth and
supple.

5. Give yourself a weekly manicure to keep
your hands and nails in perfect shape all through
waiting for baby. And if you can afford it, treat
yourself to a professional manicure and pedicure
at least one time in the last trimester. You deserve
to be pampered.

Bath Formulas for Relaxation

Again, unless your doctors says there are contraindications to bathing, until the last few months it's usually
safe to take a bath. Here are two beautiful relaxing
baths you might want to baby yourself in.

MILK BATH: This is pure luxury and why not. You'll
need at least two gallons of milk to do it. You might
economize with a package of dry powdered milk and
use the right proportions to get two gallons. And if
you don't want to economize, then by all means use
two gallons of real milk, plus two packets of milk
powder added to a 1/4 tub of warm bathwater. Then
find some fresh rose or other fragrant flower and tear
the petals up and sprinkle all over the bathwater to
add a loving touch. Now, don't you feel just like Cleo-

patra? Go on, soak it up for at least ten full and relaxing minutes. You deserve to baby yourself.

OIL BATH: Draw your regular bathwater, then add to it at least 1 cup of apricot kernel, avocado, or sesame seed oil, or if you're very budget-conscious, you can use safflower oil. Allow yourself at least ten minutes soaking time, then soap up with a gentle cleanser like Johnson's Baby Soap or Neutrogena and enjoy the soothing lubricating feel of all the oil and soap and water. Rinse off gently, allowing the oily beads to cling where they will, and if you'd like, damp-dry only enough to keep from catching a draft, but not enough to wipe all that oily residue off your body.

Treating All of You

Your body is covered with skin. And it will do some stretching as you and the baby grow. Some women swear by cocoa butter, that using this on the abdomen, on the breasts, can alleviate some of the stretch marks that are usually the result of carrying a baby. We're not sure. Some doctors think there is nothing one can do; others say tender loving care and constant moisturization can help. So you might as well do all you can. Pond's, Johnson & Johnson, Elizabeth Post Moisture Cream, cocoa butter—you'll find a wealth of inexpensive creams to smear on day and night that can help keep all of you as soft and lovely as you can be.

Here's a wonderful home remedy for dry-skin care that you may use all over your changing body:

BANANAS AND CREAM COOLER: Take 1 banana, mash well. Add 2 tablespoons half-and-half or light cream. Then add 2 tablespoons cooled strong tea brew. Finally, 1/8 cup witch hazel. Mix all these ingredients gently, hand-stirring them to a smooth, uniform consistency. You now have a lovely, cooling, protein-rich lotion. Apply to face, neck, shoulders, arms, legs, abdomen, buttocks, and back. If you need more as you grow, double the recipe. Allow this to stay on about ten to fifteen minutes, then sponge off with room-temperature water, or take a light and refreshing shower. By the way, this home remedy is excellent for use after sunning, pregnant or not.

Making Up Your Face

Your face will fill out somewhat during your pregnancy. Depending upon how much weight you do gain, and if you tend to gain it in the face and neck area, then you may have to do a bit of contouring to slim down the bloated areas. You may go back and read the contouring instructions in Chapter IV, as well as follow the special tips for a fuller face we'll give you here. The major rule to remember: Dark colors will diminish, while light and iridescents will bring forward. You'll want to use darker foundation, powder, and pencil to shade those areas that seem to be fuller, while you might add a brighter color makeup to the features that you want to play up.

- For tiny lines under the eyes, any eye bags or shadows: During pregnancy you may tend to

develop darker shadows or lines, either because
of lack of sleep or an increase in hormones.
This is temporary. All you need do is to use a
concealer—either a lighter tone foundation
base that you will apply in an inverted moon
shape to blend in under and around the eye
area, or you can choose an eye color crayon by
Aziza or Maybelline in a tone that is a bit
lighter than your own face color. Maybelline,
Cover Girl, Tangee, Bonne Bell, Colláge, all
make concealer colors in creamy foundations
and in eye crayons and shadows that will work,
depending upon your skin type. (See Chapter
IV on how to contour for further product
names.)

To apply, be sure to gently pat on with your
fingers, starting from the outer corner of your
under-eye area and going all the way to the inner corner of your nose. You may also want to
blend the half-moon up to the sides of the
bridge of your nose and in the inner eye socket.
Foundation? It can be your best friend, that is,
if it's the proper kind. Remember, it's meant to
be a second skin, and that means suggested and
not seen. Therefore it should never be cakey,
opaque, in any manner or form heavy. And at
all costs avoid those harsh edges where the
foundation ends and bare skin begins.

Whatever form of foundation you use—liquid,
cream, gel or cake, should complement your
skin tone. If your complexion is ivory, don't
pick an olive shade, even if you want to
look like you're suntanned. Do choose a color
that matches your skin tone, or slightly lighter

or darker, but only slightly. Maybelline, Cover Girl, Colláge, Angel Face, Pond's—there are a host of inexpensive foundations you'll find at the dimestore and discount store. The key: To find the proper one for your skin's oiliness and/or dryness, which may change with each month.

- Blusher: That hollow-cheeked look is definitely out while pregnant. Besides, your cheeks will probably be at their fullest. So instead of trying to create false high cheekbones, try for a more wholesome, round-cheeked rosiness. Smile wide, then apply the blusher of your choice to the fullest part of your cheek. Then brush a bit on your chin and forehead for a pretty glow that looks healthy, not made up.

- Eyeliner? Hard, straight lines circling the eyes are definitely out, and so are little wings going up at the outer corners. If you feel that your eyes are small and need definition and want to use eyeliner, fine. But then use a pencil crayon gently, and smudge the line with a finger or a cotton-tip swab afterward. If your eyes are close set, try lining the outer half only.

- Eye shadow: Of course you should read the section on makeup of the eyes for in-depth ideas. But during pregnancy you should avoid any iridescent colors, which can be damaging, as they contain harsh additives. You're probably best working with clear violets and mauves, rosy browns and taupes. You might also experiment by using as many as three different colors on the lids, blending them subtly so the color differences aren't obvious.

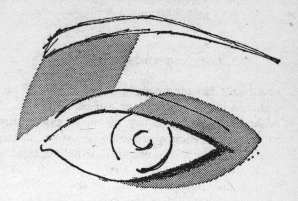

Experiment with a combination like violet and brown—violet on the inner half of the lid, brown on the outer half, blended beyond the edge of the eye. It can look very pretty, yet subdued, a look you'll want to encourage during approaching motherhood.

- Mascara: Lots of mascara is still the basic beauty rule. What to look out for is using old mascara. It can collect bacteria. Any mascara more than six months old should be discarded. Try a softer color, a brown-black or a charcoal, and see if it isn't more flattering to your face.
- Eyebrows: If you're into very thin eyebrows, they're really out. Today it's *au naturel*—little tweezing, and just some brushing. Of course if you have a hairy middle on the bridge of your nose, that should go. If you must tweeze, try using ice first to desensitize the area. And do it gently.

The Sun and Your Skin

If you didn't already know it, and I've already mentioned it in this guide, sunning can be harmful to the skin. And during pregnancy, if you're experiencing any skin discoloration, you can do permanent damage if you don't take extra precautions before exposing yourself to the sun's ultraviolet rays, which have a noxious influence that can destroy skin protein and produce an "elastosis" or stretching of the skin. The end result: wrinkling, or worse, skin cancer. And during your pregnancy, when there is greater likelihood of changes in skin pigmentation, sunning may create uneven hyperpigmentation.

The answer: moderation and protection. Always use the highest sun-blocking cream you can, like one made by Bain De Soleil or Coppertone, and sun only before ten and after three in the summer months. Don't be deluded by cloudy, foggy, or overcast days, for these too can produce severe burns, since the rays are scattered in what is called "sky radiation."

Altitude is another danger factor; the higher you are, the less atmosphere to filter the burning rays—and snow may reflect eighty-five percent of them. As for the sand, it also reflects light. And contrary to common opinion, water doesn't reflect the ultraviolet rays. They're transmitted to your body under the water—be it pool, lake, or sea. If you'll look back to Chapter VI, you'll find a list of high-protection sun products you'll find at most chain and discount stores.

A Hairy Tale

Many women find that during pregnancy they have sprouted some odd hairs on their chin, nipples, or in a strange pattern covering their diaphragm and abdomen. This can be more than disconcerting, especially if the hairs are dark and cast shadows. Never tweeze these superfluous hairs. If you do, you'll be stimulating further hair growth and distorting the base, or hair follicle, which leads to a newer and stronger and coarser regrowth. Cut them gently or you may bleach them using a very mild solution of bicarbonate of soda with a teaspoon of peroxide and soap powder mix.

The only permanent method of hair removal is electrolysis. However, it's also possible that after the baby is born the hair will fall off naturally. Some superfluous hair ceases its growth stage in direct result to the hormonal changes during pregnancy. Those that are permanent will be there three or more months after delivery. You might then want to investigate electrolysis, which is easy, and the only permanent way of freeing yourself of any embarrassing hair growth. There are electrologists in every major city and town.

Halitosis

You're going through changes and even your breath could temporarily reflect this. Also, if oral hygiene is neglected, bacteria lodge in and between the teeth and form a nearly invisible odor-causing film. Another form of bad breath that many women experience is often referred to as "morning breath." This is caused from a lack of salivary flow during sleeping hours. Brushing your tongue before bed, as well as brushing your teeth, will help here, for the tongue can become coated with food traces.

Here are some other helpful breath-cleaning tips for when you can't get to a quick toothpaste and brush cleansing.

1. Eat a crisp fresh fruit or vegetable such as apples or carrots that can temporarily help, but remember the fruit or vegetable particles left in your mouth can cause odors of their own. Rinse with water as soon as you can.

2. Try to carry a small plastic container that contains a mix of at least a tablespoon of baking soda to half a glass of water. This makes the best mouthwash/gargle for temporarily covering up bad breath.

3. Try rubbing a lemon up and down on your teeth—this helps remove some stains and surface particles. Then rinse well with water.

FOR THE OVERWEIGHT WOMAN

Positive Body Language

So you're overweight. Whether you're an emotional eater who allows an event to trigger an overeating escapade, often called a binge, or a compulsive overeater, where food is constantly on your mind, or if your build and genetic makeup are such that practically no matter what you do, you're always going to look a bit plumper than you like, you have a bit of a shaping-up problem. But you're not alone. Overeating is an American disease.

If you are in fact more than ten pounds over what is considered average weight for a woman of your height and age, then you are considered in the obese category. A good medical checkup and talk with your physician may uncover any medical problems, and if they don't exist, the opportunity of getting from a doctor the proper and sensible diet that you may safely follow would be a really good idea. There are also many excellent self-help groups that learn how to deal with the psychological outlet of eating as a response to feelings of anger, hostility, depression, and rejection. Overeaters Anonymous is one such excellent organization that is entirely free of cost, and that holds meetings in every state in our nation.

Exercise, even if it is daily walking, can help stimulate your system and inspire you to want to take off any excess weight. Lethargy, boredom, a difficult emotional period, all of these emotion-provoking situations can lead to an overweight body. It is up to you to do what you can to help get that weight off safely and slowly. Remember, slow is always better, for more than likely you're eating out of habit and not hunger, and using food as a diversion.

What to do while you're overweight to look your best? Well, there are certain rules that you may follow to shape up, to look as sensationally sexy, as pretty and slim as you can.

You can change your impact on others by altering your clothes, makeup, and hairstyle. You can cause an even greater but more subtle change by altering your mannerisms and body language. Start by becoming aware of what has positive and negative effects, then work to change those in yourself that you do find to be negative (and which, in fact, can be part of the reasons that you're eating more than your body needs, and are therefore overweight) .

Negative body language usually involves tension, a rigid, tight posture, tense hand or leg movements, such as fidgeting or patting your foot. Eye contact, an open, relaxed posture, and a sense of attention and alertness are positive body mannerisms. You'll find that changing this body language involves you in a constructive cycle. As you become more positive in your approach toward others, their response gives you more positive feedback, making it easier and easier for you to feel good about yourself. **Go on, try it. Practice makes perfect.**

Calorie Count

Whether you gain or lose weight is strictly a matter of balancing calories with activity. You'll be a better judge of whether you're eating too much or too little if you're aware of how many calories certain activities burn up. Remember, if you're tall or overweight, the same activity burns up more calories for you than a smaller person. Here are some figures for a woman of average height and weight (five feet six inches and 128 pounds). From this you can figure out what you can do and what it will do for you.

Activity	Calories per Hour
Sitting in a class or an office	80
Bicycling, moderate	215
Dancing, contemporary style	225
Housework, active	225
General calisthenics	270
Jogging, moderate	456
Swimming	480
Tennis	600
Running, active	798

A Quick Guide to Holiday Eating

Sure, you're good all year and you've lost your weight, but here come the holidays, and you're off again. A string of parties can make your eating habits slip from sensible to erratic. Faced with a buffet table of temptations, you feel out of control, saying, "Oh, I'll diet tomorrow."

What to do? A healthy diet with success potential should be able to bend with the seasons. It should have the flexibility to allow you to eat some holiday foods while you cut back on others. But if you can't juggle the calories to stay within a 1,200-a-day limit (about the most you can consume and still lose), you may be better off taking a diet vacation. In other words allow yourself a few extras during the holidays, but brush up on your holiday calorie counts first: nibble the crudités without the dip and save at least 100 calories; have turkey without gravy and save another 100; skip the butter on the sweet potatoes and cut 200. And so on. Try it, it just might work. And of course, go buy yourself a good pocket calorie counter that you'll find in many book stores, to keep a watch on how fattening those few cheese puffs could be.

Contouring Tips

Contouring is what can help you during your overweight period, especially if you have gained a considerable amount of weight in your neck and the face area. By contouring certain areas, you will achieve a slimming effect, by playing down certain features and playing up others. Since light comes forward and dark recedes, when contouring, try to achieve what one would consider a structurally beautiful face. That is, high cheekbones, a strong forehead, and a strong chin.

● Always use quick brush strokes. First, suck in the cheeks, and see the hollow contour lines on each side of the mouth. Now, take a long-handled brush and using a red-brown contour powder (Maybelline and Cover Girl are just two brands that have these colors in eye shadows and blushers) at approximately three inches vertically—below the end of each eye-ball, brush the powder outward, to the lower ear.

- Follow up with a colored blusher, preferably matching whatever color you will wear on your lips. Usually a bright and healthy-appearing color to contrast with the red-brownish contouring powder is best. Try pinks, pinky red, or anything orangy. Apply the blusher on each cheekbone, just above the red-brown contour powder, and vertically, below the end of each eyeball once again, using this as a guideline. Work the blusher into a crescent shape all the way to the temple. Blend well.

- If you have jowls or a double chin (any area that is unattractive or protruding), use some red-brown contour powder once again. Gently stroke it along either side of the neck, just under the chin, and then proceed with a horizontal stroke under the chin and across where a man's Adam's apple would be. Now lightly brush whatever red-brown contour powder is left on the brush onto your temples. Again, blend well to avoid any harsh edges.

- Next, take a wider brush with some translucent loose powder (Pond's, Cover Girl, Lady Esther, are just some of the inexpensive brands that carry this type), and brush it all over your entire face and neck. Carefully blend the contour powder so one cannot note the demarcation that can show where the contour was used under the translucent loose powder.

- Red-brown contour powder is also an excellent shadow for the eyes, and will give you a look of

depth. Or you can also use a taupe or deep
charcoal gray to diminish any fatty areas about
the eyes.

- Concealer cream or a lighter foundation can be
used to disguise any eye bags or pouches or
shadows; just be certain it isn't too light a
shade and doesn't stand out from the rest of
your makeup.

Oily-Skin Problems

Often overweight women find that they have oily
skin. It might be diet or hormones or a combination.
Check with a dermatologist if you find excessive oiliness that causes you any adult acne or other skin problems. Aside from this, you should avoid harsh soaps
and alcohol-based products, which, ironically, will
only stimulate the oil glands to produce more.

Try gently medicated soaps, like Cuticura and
Noxzema. They usually have the active ingredients
that help clean up any troublesome bacteria on your
skin. Using a witch hazel wash as an astringent will
also give you some relief. And of course, if you're
bingeing on French fries and chocolate sundaes—well,
you may now know where the problem really is.

A Natural Healer

A wonderful tonic, whose uses are innumerable as a
laxative, natural diuretic, and to relieve irritations of

the stomach and intestines is the bitter herb, golden-seal, also called yellow root, ground raspberry, and even by the unpronounceable name of *hydrastis rhizoma*. This herb grows in the well-drained woodlands of North Carolina, east of the Mississippi, and in the Pacific Northwest region. Its roots and stems are ground for use and its uses are many. You can add 1 or 2 tablespoons of the herb to 2 quarts of water and then keep it for later use. Ideally, an ounce of powder will last an entire family for several months. Of course, as with any tonic, do not abuse it. A little goes a long way. Here, just some of its applications:

- Mouthwash: Combine some of the solution with bicarbonate of soda and water. It is said to help heal gums, throat, and sores of the mouth.
- Hay fever: Snuffing a small amount of the dry powder may alleviate some of the inflammation and distress of hay fever.
- Small cuts and abrasions: Alleviate by soaking the affected area in a solution of goldenseal.
- Water retention: This is usually a problem in overweight. Of course, cut out salt. This is usually the cause. Check with your doctor if you tend to swollen ankles or wrists; it could be serious.

With the goldenseal, take a teaspoon of the powder and steep in 1 quart of boiling water. Use it as a diuretic tea for the natural release of excess water in the tissues. By the way, this is especially good for use in the premenstrual cycle.

You can purchase goldenseal in herb shops, vitamin

centers, or health-food stores, and in some larger five and dime chains. Store it in an airtight container and do keep it out of the reach of children. And remember, use it in moderation.

FOR BLACK WOMEN

Face Makers

Black women need special beauty products for their specific beauty needs. We selected a few of the most effective brands you can find in the dime and discount store and have used these in this chapter to give you customized tips. From Posner Custom Blends carried at Woolworth's, K marts, and Caldors, and other chain stores, to Revlon's Polished Ambers Collection, which you'll find discounted in many outlets like Walgreen's and Duane Reade drugstores in the East, to a new line called Honey & Spice, to Bonne Bell's complete collection of beauty products for black women found in the Midwest and West, there is no lack of choices for you to make. What you do want to know is what choices best suit your skin and hair.

Remember then, that your skin complexion is important. Actually there are as many as forty different shades of black skin, so you'll have to use the trial-and-error method of trying various foundation tones on to find what makeup shade is expressly for you. Coordination according to skin tone, and the proper blending

and contouring will be your guidelines. Don't settle
for any shades that don't bring out the best in you.
With all the manufacturers who have made complete
makeup lines just for your special coloring, there's no
reason not to shop around and test each product before buying.

Your Skin

It may be oily or dry or combination. Look at the
chapter devoted to skin types, Chapter III, and you'll

be able to ascertain just what your skin profile is. The actual care of black skin is not different from caring for any skin—it's a matter of the proper cleansing procedure and what treatment techniques and products are most effective. However, you want to be a bit more careful in removing all traces of your cleansers—be it soap, liquid remover, or astringent—to make sure that you leave a clear complexion, with no ashiness or residue.

Your skin is able to be exposed to sun a bit longer if it is a dark brown because the increased melanin of black skin will screen out the more harmful rays. Still, this doesn't mean to sun without protection, and you would be wise to use a sunscreen if you want to prolong your good looks as long as nature intended.

On Your Hair

As black women already know, their hair is particularly fragile. Hot-combing or chemical-relaxing will leave it oily, while its natural curliness leads to tangling and hair breakage. Therefore you should take extra care in the styles you choose to wear, and if you can, select a natural haircut and easy style that won't need much treatment.

You also need good conditioners, special shampoos, and coloring products. L'Oréal has a complete line called Radiance that offers such products as The Penetrating Conditioning Treatment, a thirty-minute treatment for damaged hair, and a Special Cleansing Shampoo for all black hair types.

Since black hair can be especially hard to shampoo

because its texture and curl make it tangle so easily, you'd do well to try out a number of brands like L'Oréal shampoos, Breck, and Jheri Redding, until you find one that penetrates the hair shaft, that offers a mild, pH-balanced formula, and gives you a deep and gentle cleansing. In this case, try to buy those small sample sizes that are offered in drugstores and chains, and try a few until you achieve the results you want.

You would do well to check with a specialist in hair-coloring if you decide to color your hair. Black hair is wiry, and in some cases is resistant to color change, and can break. Conventional hair dyes usually prove unsatisfactory. There are many black hairdressers and salons that specialize in coloring your type of hair, and, so it is a worthwhile investment to seek professional advice and treatment.

If your hair is healthy, and you have tried a sample swatch of hair as a trial, then hair color is indeed possible. There are conditioning ingredients in most hair-color products that will protect your hair. If you use a relaxer on the hair, most experts advise that you wait at least six weeks after a relaxing treatment before coloring.

Shampoo-in hair colors made by Clairol and L'Oréal and Roux can also improve the look of your hair; it adds rich tones and highlights to unexciting natural hair color, enhances your complexion, and if you're beginning to gray, coloring can subtract years from your appearance.

To determine which hair-color shade you should select, it's helpful to first determine the natural color of your hair. In good light—preferably sunlight—make a part and examine your hair close to the scalp.

Note the highlights. Your dark brown hair may have reddish tones; black hair may have rich, brown highlights; brown or red hair may have winey auburn tones. When coloring your hair, it's often best to choose a shade that complements your hair's natural color and highlights.

Consider your skin tone, too, before choosing a shade. One of the best ways to decide is to try on a wig in the shade you might be considering; if it's flattering to your complexion, chances are a similar shade will also look attractive.

Before beginning any home-coloring process, do a patch test and a strand test to make sure it's the color you want and that you are not allergic to the product.

For a special guide to black hair care, L'Oréal, which makes the Radiance black hair-product line, offers a free guide.

For Dry Skin

If you suffer from dry, ashy patches, you need a rich lotion to absorb and soften this rough, dry skin. There are many good products at discount prices that can help—from Vaseline Intensive Care Lotion for Over-Dry Skin, to Pond's Dry Skin Cream to good old petroleum jelly. The trick here is to use a good enriching cream often, and all over. Make it a habit to apply and reapply moisturizers after a bath or shower, and again before bed to combat the dry-skin problem.

Keloids Are a Problem

Dr. James Reardon, a leading New York plastic surgeon, operates on many black women who seek face lifts, eye lifts, and other cosmetic corrections. He does point out the differences in black skin, and advises that there are some risks in surgery, as there are in other situations caused by accidents. The risks involve keloids, clusters of fibrous overgrowths of scar tissues that form when some black skin is cut. They can often be successfully removed through plastic surgery, however there is some reoccurrence. It's up to a physician to determine who is and isn't a good candidate.

Some keloids can also be treated by a dermatologist by shrinking the keloid tissue with an injection of medication, and you might also investigate this route if you have such scars that are unattractive and causing you discomfort.

What causes keloids? It seems to be due to a greater concentration of melanin, which is the ingredient that determines skin tones and color, in the skin of both black and oriental women, who have a higher incidence of such growths. However, even blond, fair-complexioned women can have the condition; in this case it's usually genetic.

Back to Basics

When you're ready to choose new makeup, don't buy any you can't test first. Almost all major department-store cosmetics counters have testers and people trained as "beauty advisers." Take advantage. Go and choose what you think you want, try it on, ask questions, and if you like it, you'll find it in a cheaper version later at the dimestore and discount store.

How to test makeup? If you're buying shadow, blusher, or liquid makeup, rub some on your wrist to check what is called the color release. If you have to put a lot on to match your skin tone, it's not right for you. Remember, the stronger the color you get when you first put it on, the longer it's going to last.

Staying Power

How to apply makeup that will last all day? Well, you just may not want it to remain on your face that long. If you tend to oily skin, you'll need to wash it during the day, or at the least use an astringent. A water-base makeup will wear better for you than an oily type. Some professional models carry a light container of translucent or at the least a soft beige powder along, one that blends with their foundation easily, and which helps to set the makeup. If you apply makeup carefully in the morning, and allow at least twenty minutes for precise application, more than likely the work will remain all day and you'll only need to freshen up your lip color.

If you do have oily skin, you might try an oil-blotting makeup like Maybelline's. As for washing your face, Jergens makes Wash Tub Lathering Face Wash that promises to wash away excess oil, grease, and grime. You might keep a container at the office for washing up in between.

The Magic of Makeup

Black skin can vary in color from almost the palest of rachel to a deep mahogany, all of which may complicate your selecting the proper shade of makeup and matching eye and rouge and lipstick. Some women also find that they have uneven pigmentation, which creates added problems.

No more. Manufacturers like Posner, Ultra Sheen, and Bonne Bell have created so many colors and shades expressly for black women, that you'll find those that best suit you. And if necessary you may have to use two shades to cover your complexion properly. Learning how to blend, what to use where, and how is an art.

First, makeup should match your skin exactly. Highlighting can be achieved by using lighter shades of the foundation, and contouring by choosing a darker shade. Using these simple guidelines, you can safely select not only a foundation, but the corresponding blusher.

Skin Tone:	Corresponding Shades of Foundation and Blusher:
Natural to light tan	Beige tones (without any rose or red cast) in foundation; blusher shades in pink, peach, or apricot
Medium brown	Medium-brown shade of foundation; blushers in rose or deep mauve shades
Dark brown	Rich brown shades in foundation; blushers in burgundy, bronze, or deep red
Deep ebony	Dark shades of foundation; blusher in burgundy or rich red

Lip Trips

You may find some uneven tones in your lips—from pink to dark brown. What you have to do is first even out the spotted tones by using your foundation as a concealing cream base. Then, if you have full lips, remember to draw a line inside your natural line to narrow the fullness a bit. If you have very full lips, you might want to use a gloss instead of color. For narrow lips, do the opposite, and make the outline with your pencil or lipstick brush outside the natural line to widen the illusion.

Bronzing Gels

Bonne Bell, one of the many manufacturers who have created an entire line of products for black women, has an excellent bronzing gel that can give a natural, healthy look to black skin. What's more, you can use the gel alone, or as a blending agent to achieve a desired shade for your specific skin tone. For instance, if you have a sallow or ruddy complexion, you can add highlights with the gel. Also, it's suitable for all skin types—dry, normal, oily, or combination.

Coty has a Glowing Finish Bare Blusher that can add highlights. Aziza makes a Natural Glow Powder Blush that works well on oily skins too.

Kohl

It was once used by Cleopatra, and today kohl comes in many shades, all in pencil form, and perfect for eyeliner. For instance you'll find charcoal, black, and dark brown kohl in eye pencils in many five and dime stores. Choose the color that matches your eyelid color, then line the inner rim of your eyes for drama and definition. And finish off with mascara. A darker color on your upper lashes and a lighter one on your lowers will avoid casting shadows on your darker-toned skin and can also serve to brighten up the eyes.

Posner makes a complete line of eye-makeup products that are specifically created for a black woman's beauty regimen.

For THE MATURE WOMAN

Winning the Age Game

You're not getting older, just better. The timeless essentials—self-esteem, sex appeal, and a healthy prettiness—are absolutely invaluable if you want to evolve into one of those ageless sexy women who keep on looking better and better. And why not. Care, taking time to learn and to continue to grow, and to correct whatever premature aging signs nature may create, knowing how to use makeup properly—all of this adds up to an even more positive and beautiful you.

Facing It

What you need is a long-range regimen for healthy, supple skin. If there's one area of beauty and grooming which invariably causes confusion among women, it's skin care. And that concern increases as skin matures. There are no easy answers to skin problems because each individual is born with certain genetic pluses as well as the inevitable minuses. Of course,

skin care is best begun when we're young. But it's not too late, ever, to do the best for you that you can.

Just what are the best things a woman of forty and over can do to keep her skin looking as young as possible for as long as possible?

First, use a sun block whenever you're out in the sun. You should also avoid overdrying of the skin. Air conditioning, overheated homes and windy or dry weather all dehydrate the skin. Wetting it sufficiently before applying your moisturizer will also help your makeup to look smoother and will aid the moisturizer in working better. And don't be misled by the claims in advertising you'll find all over the magazines and newspapers. Skin-care products are not the miracles the manufacturers say they are. You'll find just as much value in a jar of Pond's skin cream as you will in the far more expensive forty-five-dollar jar that is touted in full-page ads as being worn by women in the know. Nonsense. If you'll learn how to sensibly use products, and use them on a daily basis, you'll do just as well with a lubricating oil that costs two dollars as one that costs twenty dollars and more.

You should also seek professional advice when you want answers. Cosmetic salespeople are not always the most adequate sources you might think they are and may not be trained in knowing individual answers, yet you'd be surprised how many women will follow such advice. If you have a special skin condition, for instance, then forget about using a cream the saleslady has just said will cure the ailment. Go see a dermatologist to get at the source.

Updating Your Hair

By the time a woman reaches thirty-five, she sees her first gray hair. Because the right hair color is one of the most effective deterrents to premature aging, the use of streaking or color rinsing can help. In this case you might want to seek the professional advice of a colorist at a salon. You could also invest in a professional coloring treatment until you're used to the new look, and can do it yourself at home, if that's what would most please your budget.

Hair begins to lose pigment around thirty-five. Skin

tone and eye color also get a bit drabber. After your thirties, if you have a yellow color hair, you'll need a more precise, softer color with gradations in it. Opt for tawniness or an ash-blond shade made by L'Oréal or Clairol, for gold or yellow make skin look sallow rather than peachy and glowing. It's also important to consider the lighting—do you work in a fluorescent setting? Color variations are affected also by our environment.

Whatever color hair you may consider changing to, avoid the real reds. After the thirties, hair and skin fades and red is the hardest color there is both to wear and to maintain. Also, avoid any harsh colors.

The Gray Hair Question

Yes, you can be prematurely gray, and if you insist that natural is better and want to remain that way, fine. But you will look older. When a man grays he feels distinguished; most women feel older. If you only have a few gray hairs, you can warm them up or brighten them by using a frosting kit from Clairol, L'Oréal, or Revlon, to name just a few. However, if you have dark brown hair and a few grays coming in, you might want to consult with a color expert at your local salon. Ask just what shades of color will work best into the hair highlights. There are many types of streaking and highlighting that are being done professionally today. Most are quite flattering.

To Rinse or Not

Nestle's started it, those color rinses you'll still find in the dimestore. And yes, they can work out just fine. If all you want to do is brighten or temporarily color your hair and add some luster, then try out one of the many color rinses you'll find at the chain and discount stores. A rinse will wash out gradually, and can last three to four weeks.

Hairstyles for You

Hair fashions change from year to year. So do you. As you age, long hair looks less flattering. It tends to draw the focus of attention down, like drooping lines; down is not as positive as a shorter cut, perhaps just below the chin, or halfway to your neck. Try to choose a style that is both compatible with your age and most flattering. This may mean that an off-the-face look can be an advantage. A longer-than-shoulder length style will more than likely make you look older, not younger. And of course, that overly bleached-blond look you wore in your twenties is a no-no today. Remember, you want to draw attention to the all of you, not one part.

The Gentle Way of Cleansing Your Face

No matter one's age, everyone can have a clear skin, pore-deep clean, which means it should be free of the ravages of pollution, the city grime, and the country dust. And it doesn't cost a lot of money and investing in those professional facials. All it takes is time and patience. You can do a perfectly wonderful facial steaming at home. Here's how and what you'll need.

Equipment Needed:
> 3 quart pot with cover
> towel
> a handful of dried herbs, like rosemary, thyme and chamomile
> ½ quart of spring water, or mineral water
> ⅓ quart of tap water that you have allowed to sit in an open bottle for 24 hours (to remove impurities like chlorine)

Directions for Giving Yourself a Facial Steaming:
STEP 1. Gently wash your face well, leaving it moist.
STEP 2. Drop at least a handful of herbs (rosemary, thyme, or chamomile, which you can buy at the health-food shop or even in some supermarkets) into the pot, then add the two half quarts of water. Cover the pot.
STEP 3. Set on a medium heat setting and bring to a boil. Then lower the heat and simmer for

about five minutes more to allow the dried herbs to yield all their essences.

STEP 4. Now, turn off the heat, and remove the pot to a table.

STEP 5. Cover your hair with a turban, or tie it back.

STEP 6. With a good-sized (bath or large hand) towel, cover your head and the pot by making a sort of a tent, and then remove the lid from the pot allowing the fragrant steam to rise up onto your face. By the way, if you have very sensitive skin, back away from the pot at least twelve inches so that your skin doesn't get too hot or feel uncomfortable. In any case, don't be more than eight inches from the steam.

STEP 7. Allow this herbal steam to drift toward your face with your eyes closed for at least ten minutes, rotating your face as you do this.

STEP 8. Once you have steamed your face in this manner, you will open the pores and rid the skin of toxins and impurities. You should follow this with a warm rinse, finally a truly cold splash of water done at least a half dozen times to act as an astringent and to begin closing the pores. It will take as long as an hour before the pores fully contract.

STEP 9. Use your favorite moisturizing cream in those areas that are most sensitive and need it, like about the eyes and above the lips, and on the neck. The moisturizer will absorb so much faster while your pores are open.

STEP 10. Wait at least a half hour before applying any foundation or powder to give your face a rest.

The Over-Forty Yeast Mask

Sometimes what you need is a good and nourishing facial mask to perk your skin up and give it some stimulation. Here is an excellent at-home facial that costs a bit to make but has a wonderfully effective result for skin that is on the aging side. Try it out and see how well it works for you. It should replenish dried-out skin as well as help add topical nourishment to oily and combination skin. Use it at least once weekly for optimal results.

>   1 tablespoon plain yogurt
>   1 tablespoon brewer's yeast powder
>   1 capsule each: vitamin D (5,000 units) vitamin
>   A, (5,000 units), vitamin E (400 units)

Now, mix all the above ingredients gently together until a paste has been formed. Apply to your face, avoiding only the eyes but using gently around them. Allow it to remain on at least twenty minutes, or until the mask is completely dry. Then wash face with lukewarm water only until the mask is removed completely. After, pierce another capsule of the vitamin E (400-unit size) and use this to treat the delicate skin areas about the eyes and around the nasal-labial lines (that run from nose to mouth) as well as on your neck. Dab on gently and allow to remain at least a half hour; then remove any residue with a tissue, although you can allow a film to remain, before you have to apply any makeup.

Note: If you will use this treatment faithfully your skin will look and feel younger and respond to the care you are giving it.

Your Hands

You can tell little white lies about your age if you care to, but your hands, at least the back of them, will give you away. Pamper them with isotonic gloves like those made by Aris—even sleep with them. And be sure to wear rubber or vinyl gloves whenever you are washing dishes or doing any manual labor. For all the care you give your hands at night will be wasted if you neglect them during the day. Well-manicured hands with a bit of bright polish can do much for a feminine look. So will properly pedicured toes. (You'll find complete instructions on how to give yourself a manicure and pedicure in Chapter V.)

Liver Spots

Those brownish spots that develop as we age are rather normal, if unsightly. It's genetic and not much can be done to reverse them or remove them. Bleaching lotions are generally unsafe and many women are allergic to some of the ingredients that are in them, like quinine. Often found on the backs of hands, "liver spots" is the common name for skin discoloration. It's caused by a disturbance of melanin, the substance which controls the skin's pigmentation. Staying out of the sun will help, as the ultraviolet rays stimulate their emergence. (By the way, they can be removed by a chemical peeling process as practiced by plastic surgeons.)

From Nefertiti to Now

Makeup has always been a magic ingredient for women from times gone by right to this very moment.

Defined cheekbones, the proper eye look, a long neck, pretty lips, a strong chin—there are certain values most societies hold that don't change. However, what does are the fashions in makeup, from thin arched eyebrows to those heavy false eyelashes to a good dab of fuchsia lipstick to pale pink colors on, you can almost always approximate the time a movie was made from the style of a woman's makeup and hair.

Like most women over forty, you may be using either too much or not enough makeup. It's not always easy to find the happy medium, to change with the times, to know that the eyebrows you wore at twenty-five just don't look attractive now when natural is in and your face has changed. Many makeup manufacturers provide personal makeup sessions when they want to introduce a new product. Makeup artists appear in department stores and often will give you a free lesson. Look in the newspapers for upcoming events and take the time to attend one of these sessions whenever you can. You can always learn something new, and then copy until perfect at home.

It is up to you to experiment with foundation, cheek color, eye shadow, liner, and mascara by using the information provided in this book. Remember, the effect you want should always be a soft and natural one, never obvious. Patience and practicing until you've mastered the art it takes to play up your most beautiful features and play down the rest will indeed pay off. It's an "accent the positive, eliminate the negative" routine you're after.

Designing a New Face

It takes time. And practice. But it's possible. Determining the right colors and the types of foundation and powders and rouges that are exactly you may mean several trips to the dimestore and even purchasing a product that later on just doesn't measure up to your expectations. But you're after a look that is natural and lovely and that makes you glow. It will be well worth all the effort you invest in the matter.

First, determine the type of foundation you can wear. If you'll figure out your facial type in Chapter III, then try on both water-base and oil-base foundations to learn which looks the best and has the most staying power, you'll learn firsthand what effect each has on your skin. If the color turns, for instance, then your skin may have an oily residue that just doesn't work with that particular brand or type of base. Or if you wear a foundation that seems right but later on you feel a parched, drawing sensation, then this makeup might be too dry for your skin. And so on.

The same principle of selection works with powders, rouges, eye shadows, and eye crayon pencils. Trying them on, seeing how they work on your face, is really the best criterion for deciding what products to buy. What you might do is borrow makeup from a friend who has a similar coloring to yours and see how her eyeliner looks on your eyes, and so forth. Some women have arranged their own weekly makeup club where they can exchange ideas and products and tips. Perhaps you can meet with a few friends and do the same.

It's a good way to save money and learn what is newest on the market without having to buy a hundred different items to get the few that work best for you.

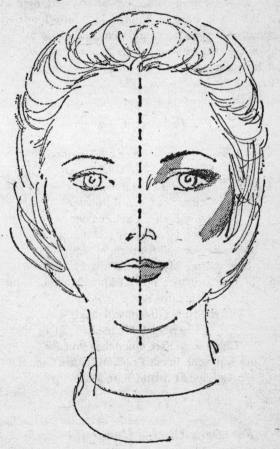

Once you've chosen your makeup base, and are ready to apply it over your clean and moisturized face, do it using your fingertips, blending the foundation

upward and outward toward the sides of your face. Be
sure to cover under the jawline so you don't have any
harsh edges showing. The major rule here: Always
choose a color foundation closest to your own skin
tone. What you want to do is add a subtle foundation
to smooth out your pores and give you a base of operation for the rest of your makeup, not to create a new
color for your face.

Product Cues

Some Foundations and Powders
Max Factor Moist Makeup
Angel Face Powder
Constance Carroll Powder
Lady Esther Face Powder
Revlon Moisturizing Makeup
Revlon Oil-Blotting Makeup
Maybelline Moisture Whip Make-Up
Maybelline Moisture Whip Liquid Make-Up and
Moisture Whip Powder
Maybelline Oil-Control Make-Up
Chap Stick Make-Up
Chap Stick Face Quencher Powder
Coty Equasion Fresh Peach Moisture Cream
Colláge Moisture Base Make-Up

For Dark Circles Under the Eyes

A shade of foundation about two shades lighter than
the all-over base you're already using makes an excel-

lent concealing cream. Here is one area where cream works well without any powder. Powdering will only create dry and lined looks so avoid using it in any sensitive area like under or around the eyes. Use an inverted crescent shape to obliterate any dark circles with the lighter shade foundation, making sure to blend it well. And of course, if you're not getting enough rest, make sure to sleep as much as you can.

Drooping Eyelids

One of the first signs of aging appear around the eyes and usually manifest themselves in a sleepy look caused by an overly hanging upper eyelid. Of course, you may consider cosmetic surgery, which is becoming quite popular today and less costly. This will be the only permanent method of removing those excessive lines and baggy looks. In the meanwhile, makeup can camouflage, if used properly.

First, widen the eye shadow that you are using all over your eyelids to the outer corners and extend the shadow on an upward slant which will deflect the focus from the downward curve. Using an eyelash curler will also help this problem. By the way, choosing a deep brown or a taupe shade of shadow will help the over-hanging lid to recede a bit.

Don't Pout

Old-fashioned colors are one of the best ways to date yourself. If you're still hanging on to that Tangee bright orange from high-school days, forget it. Orange is too glaring and is out. What you want is a natural, soft look, and your lipstick is one way of reflecting that. Better to only use gloss in a berry or soft red color than to add too much blue or orange or obviousness to your lips.

You should also consider a wardrobe of lipstick colors to go with your fashions. And of course, match lipstick to nail-polish color. Cutex, Maybelline, Collage, Cover Girl, are some of the manufacturers who make coordinated lip and nail colors. And you'll also find a wealth of glosses that also mix and match with ease. Your eye makeup should also coordinate, meaning that you won't want to wear a bright pink lipstick if your eyes are wearing a brown eye shadow, when really, wearing a violet eye shadow will pick up the pink and vice versa. In other words, always think of the total look, and make sure that all your makeup is in harmony.

Before applying lipstick, dust your lips lightly with some talc or translucent powder. Then your lipstick brush should be used to outline the lips properly. Finally, fill in the outline with whatever color you have chosen to wear that will blend with the rest of your makeup. Now add a bit of a shiny, lustrous lip gloss. A moist mouth always has a youthful appeal. And carry some gloss along with you for freshing up and keeping your lips dewy appealing.

Special Beauty Problems and Their Solutions

THE CHIN: If your chin is a part of a too-prominent jawline, or a too-round face, apply a dark blusher by Cover Girl or Max Factor, for instance, to the jawbone. If your chin recedes, you can bring it forward by highlighting it with a lighter shade of foundation. If you have a pointed chin, you can correct it by contouring with a foundation or a blusher in a deeper color. Some foundations that come in dark and light shades that you might like are made by Revlon, Max Factor, and Bonne Bell, and come in liquid and in cream forms. Try them out first, before you buy.

THE FOREHEAD: If yours is too high, to shorten it, use a foundation several shades darker in color than your usual. Apply it from the hairline to the middle of the forehead. Blend well. And, of course, bangs are always in and can add a youthful look. If you have a narrow forehead, you can widen it by using a lighter shade of foundation at each temple.

THE NOSE: If your nose happens to be too short, add length by highlighting the whole nose, plus the tip. Blend well. If it's too wide, then narrow down by contouring it at the sides with a deeper shade of the same foundation you use for concealing. If your nose is too large, powder is a great help. It dulls the shine, thus putting less emphasis on a prominent nose. And if your nose isn't straight enough, shade the crooked side, while highlighting the other. Blend a line of color down the middle of the nose, too, with some blusher.

MAKEUP FOR THE MOONLIGHT . . .

FOR DRESS-UP AND EVENING TIME

Putting on the Glitz

Holidays. Party. Weddings. Showers. Engagements. Birthdays. Disco! Ballroom Dancing. Dressing up and going out to celebrate is what all of these occasions are all about. This is the time to pull out all stops on how you look, because you can bedazzle with a bright hairstyle, add glamour to the event and yourself by putting on makeup with an accent. It's your time to be the woman of the hour and feel it.

Looking terrific is especially important at dress-up time. When it's in the evening, you know that the artificial lighting means wear more instead of less, which applies to your makeup as well as your clothes. Nothing makes a woman feel quite so alluring as dressing up and going out, of feeling that she looks very special. How? By taking all the tips on contouring and eye looks and hair and using them now, with the new looks that are highlighted here.

Hair by Candlelight

It's nighttime and you're going somewhere special. What you want is a glamorous hairdo that will do something special too. It really doesn't matter if you have short, medium, or long hair—you can easily transform it into an elegant style punctuated with only a few differences from your regular daytime look. For instance, if you have long hair, you can put it up in braids or a chignon, then add a bow or two in the color that matches your outfit. If it's short or medium, you might add a bright barrette or two combs to sweep up the hair and add some waves. After-dark hair fashions take imagination, a bit of time, and you can copy just about any super look you see in your favorite magazine. If you are dressing up for an event that is formal, and you want to imitate a favorite hair creation, ask a friend to help. In this case, four hands are better than two. Back-swept hair, intricate braiding, clipping, and chignons will work just fine if you'll use a back mirror and, when in doubt, get aid.

Here are some unique items you'll find around the house that you could use in a special hair design:

1. Glittery headband. Made out of an old beaded necklace, you can attach it to a piece of felt material, add ties to secure.

2. Metallic stars. Buy some metallic paper, cut out as star shapes, glue onto some large bobby pins, and you have instant stardom.

3. Shawl. Purchase an exotic shawl, wrap your head up like a sheik, and you'll have instant drama.

4. Bells. Buy some Christmas tinkling bells and add them to the long braid or ponytail you have swept your hair up into. You'll tinkle while you dance.

5. Feathers. Put your hair into an upsweep with

some pretty swirls and folds at the front, then add a wild feather and let it make its own fantasy statement.

6. Veils. Purchase some unusual black veiling and after you put your hair into a sleek twist, define your glamour by wrapping your head in veiling.

7. Food coloring. If you're really daring, and have light hair, you can add a few bizarre streaks of color with ordinary kitchen food colors. For instance, you can mix a purple color and add it to the front and sides of your ash-blond hair, or take some green or orange colors and add them to achieve a wild affect. Of course, use shampoo to wash out all that wild color before you go out of the house the next day. The coloring is really only for special nights.

8. Bows. Buy grosgrain ribbon or velvet ribbon (depending on the season and your fashion) and make tiny little bows that you affix to fine hairpins, then add all over your head for a wild and hatty look.

9. Flowers. Why not? Sleek back your hair with some White Rose Petroleum Jelly pomade and give it a South Seas look. Then add a wild flower or two like Dorothy Lamour wore in the old "Road" movies. Or take the flowers and make them into a circlet headband and let your hair flow loose.

10. Spray-on Colors. Nestle's is one of the makers of those spray-on colors like copper and gold you'll find in some dimestores. Use at will and randomly for a wild and dazzling look. Then shampoo out well the next day.

Body Highlighting

If you're wearing a décolletage dress, why not add some special highlighting? Blend dark makeup (powder or pancake is best, and you'll find both Max Factor and Revlon make them) in to the hollow area between the breasts with a damp sponge or fingers. Then apply light, shiny powder—one that is intended as an eye shadow—to top slope of breast. Then add a little shine to the shoulders for a sweetly rounded contour. And a sexy one.

And if you'll employ an iridescent shadow—one of those really pearly ones made by Maybelline or a gold or silver from FlameGlo—you can add highlights to elbows, knees, wherever you really want to glitter. The only limitation is your imagination. And you know you've got lots of that.

Glitter On

Other ways to add glitter to your overall makeup:

- Add complementary metallic dusts, which you can purchase from Stagelight Cosmetics, to your lip gloss and then blend into the lipstick for sparkle and shine.
- Highlight your cheeks with a fuchsia/pink rouge by Collóge or Natural Wonder. Then

add a gold star to the middle for a really glow-in-the-dark look.

- Buy some paste-on rhinestones and paste-on to your face in a beauty-spot arrangement, or add to an ankle like a bracelet.
- The new sparkle gels are also great for shoulders, arms, cheeks, and brow bones; shop around at specialty makeup shops for these, or try Colláge Gel Rouges.
- Bright primary-color shadows, such as electric turquoise, purple, hot pink, fuchsias, and those metallic crayons can be used for P.M. dressing in stripes and all-over patterns (Aziza and Maybelline).
- Gold eye shadow makes splendid highlighter. Circle the eyes from temple to cheekbone, then put a dollop on the lower lip for a pouty, sexy mouth.
- Buy gold or silver cake decoration candies and use them as the finishing touch for your hair, or paste on under one eye.

Batting an Extra Pair of Eyelashes

False eyelashes are always in fashion for a special evening. For a really dramatic eye look, you just can't afford not to have them. Maybelline, Aziza, Revlon, are just a few of the manufacturers who make them. And you will find lots of styles in your local dimestore and discount store. How to apply them and wear them with ease is what may take getting used to especially if you haven't been using them, but they're well worth the extra effort. Here's how:

1. First put some of the adhesive that comes with your eyelashes on a piece of cardboard, then close the cap to the tube. (The adhesive dries out fast.)

2. Using a tweezers, place one lash by its tip on the cardboard, near the adhesive.

3. Using a cotton swab, delicately apply the poured adhesive to the curved, pointed end of the lash, then spread it thinly all over the back of its band.

4. Holding a magnifying mirror, hold the lash in the tweezers and move it over your own lash, landing it right on top.

5. Look in the mirror, and using both hands, secure the lash and adjust it so that it slides into the little groove at the root of your own lashes.

6. Repeat this process with the second lash.

7. Using mascara, do lower lashes first, then upper, with double lashes.

Tips: The lashes should extend no farther out at the outside corners of your eye than your own lashes do. In some cases it's best if they stop a bit before your own.

If you want an even more dramatic look, you can also apply lashes to your bottom lash line. However, you need a large eye and a dress-up occasion to do it and not look overdone.

Practice makes perfect. Wear the false eyelashes around the house a few times and you'll get used to both wearing them and feeling that they are light-

weight and natural. They can become second nature
to you if you'll trim them properly, clean them properly, and if they're lightweight and not too thick or
overly defined. Strive for a glamorous look, but not a
devastating one, which means don't wear Minnie
Mouse eyelashes or any lashes that don't look fragile
and feminine. You'd be surprised how exciting false
eyelashes can appear when they are the proper size and
shape for your face and eyes. Try a few pair on and
trim or thin with scissors if the ones you have chosen
make you look too heavy-eyed.

Creating a Nighttime Face

We asked makeup artist Raphael Tosta, who does
makeup work for Stagelight Cosmetics in New York,
to create a special after-dark look that could be included in this section. Obviously the colors Raphael
suggests are only general ones. You will have to adapt
them to your own coloring, mood, and the brands you
choose to use. But if you'll follow his steps to a dress-
up face, you will have a good beginning.

- First, place a bright foundation on the face,
  one or two shades lighter than your usual
  choice, to reflect the lights of evening. Or use a
  sparkling powder over your regular foundation.
- For eyes: Use sparkling or luminescent eye
  shadow in a more vivid shade than usual. Use
  three tones of any color for a more emphasized
  shape.

- Use a midnight-blue eyeliner pencil near the lashes, then use navy blue mascara. Or if you choose to use a black eyeliner, coordinate with black mascara.
- Put a bright color lipstick, a really hot pink or wild red shade on lips. First outline with lipstick pencil, then fill in. Add a bright gloss.
- To contour the face, use three colors. The first, a neutralizer and a very light powder to place under the eyes, just above the cheekbone area. Then use the dark contouring color (at least two or three tones darker than your own skin color), to make deep shadow effects at the temples, on the sides of the nose, under the jawbone, on each side, just under the chin, and the hollow of the face between the jawbone and the cheekbone. The third color to use should be one that gives the basic color to the face, like a bright pink, so that the night lights will reflect the color. Place medium color on cheekbones in between the darker and lighter colors. Blend well.
- For eyebrows, comb and make the shape you want using a shade of eyebrow shadow that is closest to your own.

Finishing Up with Fragrance

What better time to discuss fragrance, than for dress-up? Of course, you wear your favorite cologne or perfume all day. It's the essence of femininity. But nothing is more luscious then the romance of a scent

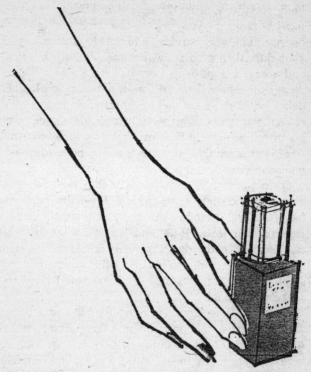

wafting lightly about you in the evening. It can be your signature, the perfect finishing touch to a beautiful you.

Fragrance comes in seven types: Single florals like Joy, floral bouquets like Arpege, spicy blends like Vetiver, forest blends like Aliage, fruity blends like Jean Naté, oriental blends like Cie, and modern blends like Estēe Lauder are examples of just a few. If that isn't confusing enough, there are even combinations of these. How to choose from this dazzling array? Since fragrance changes according to your own particular body chemistry, it won't be much help to choose a scent because it's your friend's favorite. It must work on you. The only valid way to decide is to test it on your skin, then wear it awhile, and if it still holds up and you feel good in it, buy it. First go to a department store where there are lots of testers around. Then dab a bit of the scent you are interested in on the inside of your wrist. Wait until it dries, then sniff. After about ten minutes do the sniff test again. By the way, never test more than two scents at the same time—one on each wrist—or you'll be confused.

Once you're sure that you like the fragrance, purchase it. Of course, scents change. The initial dab you have used as a test is what the professional perfumer calls the "top note." The "end" scent is what will waft up later on in the day, that is, if it mixes well with your body oils and skin and lasts that long. It is that second fragrance that should please you before you make a purchase.

Once you have found a scent that fits your image and life-style, use it. Perfume evaporates rather quickly and should be enjoyed. Like fine wines, they actually deteriorate in the bottle. Store it in the refrigerator if it's particularly precious to you, or in any cool, dark place. And of course, keep the bottle tightly stoppered.

Where to use? Dab the fragrance on the temples, wrists, throat, earlobes, palms, backs of knees, and on the hem of your dress when you're going dancing. Carry some toilet water or cologne with you to freshen up later. And do give the fragrance about twenty minutes to really "settle" before you leave for the evening. If you apply it just before going out of doors, it might leave you for the open air.

CHAPTER VIII

Home Remedies and Recipes

The Low-Cost Path to Beauty

If your mind's on saving money in these days of the dollar squeeze (and whose isn't?), then you'll want to investigate every facet of making do with budget-stretching ideas, and ways to not only spend less on products but to make some of them up yourself. Remember, there are lots of clever techniques you can learn to help you look great without spending a fortune.

There are ways to avoid buying items that only end up in the trash can after you've used them once or twice. There are also techniques to make your makeup last longer. And of course, if you learn what's for free and how to take advantage of those makeovers and samples that are available at the cosmetics counters in larger department stores, you'll be ahead of the game. Here is a list of general tips to help you get the most out of your cosmetic dollars.

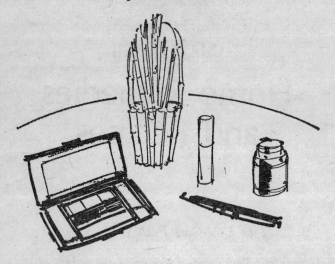

1. Make a few wise investments, like makeup brushes that help to give you that flawless look. Sable brushes in an art-supply store are perfect. Mod makes a rather inexpensive set too.

2. A simple item can get a lot of mileage if you'll adapt it for many uses. For instance, baby oil can be used to moisturize your body after a shower, as a cuticle cream, to deep condition your hair, to remove makeup, or instead of shaving cream to shave your legs. Johnson's Baby Oil or Neutrogena Natural Sesame Seed Body Oil are two products you'll find at the dimestore. And then there's always the fine vegetable oils you can purchase at the supermarket.

3. If your lipstick's down to the bottom of the tube, use a lipbrush to get the last bit out. You can actually use the same tube for weeks in this manner.

4. Do as many hairdressers do—dilute shampoo with plain water. One part shampoo to seven parts water are the proportions.

5. Buy large economy sizes of every beauty aid you can—but be sure the product's right for you or you'll waste money. Try out a sample or two first.

6. Baking soda is great for brushing the teeth and costs much less than toothpaste. At least alternate, and use it once a day.

7. Use nail thinner or paint solvent to stretch a bottle of nail polish that's gotten too thick to use anymore.

8. If your foundation is getting thick and cakey, add a few drops of water to thin it out.

9. Learn to get double usage out of a single cosmetic. Lipstick, for instance, can be used to color your cheeks and eye crayons can be smudged into shadows besides using them to line your eyes. Taupe eye shadow is excellent for contouring the face. And a pink or light shade eye crayon pencil makes a great highlighter.

10. If you're down to the last of the mascara in the tube, wet the wand with a bit of hot water before inserting it.

11. When eye shadow is old and begins to dry, apply a bit of oil to it and let it set for a day or two. This will refresh it and help it cling to the applicator better.

12. Try mixing some old colors together to see if you can come up with a new shade you like. For instance, a boring pink lipstick can be used atop a plain berry one to get a new and more dazzling look without buying a third shade.

Secrets from Mother Nature

Natural substances can work wonders because they complement and fulfill the natural requirements of your skin and hair. You'd be surprised to learn just what your kitchen staples offer. By mixing up some oatmeal, vinegar, eggs, honey, yeast, you can come up with treatments that are properly acid-balanced and also free of the additives necessary in commercial products. Not only that, but you'll be able to save lots of money by following some of these inexpensive recipes.

Remember, oftentimes the more expensive the beauty product, the more problems it can cause. The additives that are included in certain creams and lotions not only increase the cost, but can cause skin irritation. And when a product is advertised as "new and improved," it generally means that new chemicals have been added to it and that you, the consumer, will pay more for it.

It makes sense, then, to arm yourself with helpful hints, know what ingredients can do, and when you can make them up yourself. From hair rinses and colors to skin facials to body conditioners, there is nary a treatment you can't make for yourself at home.

Natural Recipes for Healthy Hair

Natural is certainly the key word for hair color. If you will use natural vegetable bleaches and organic dyes, you'll avoid those allergens in many commerical products, besides saving money. Herbs for the hair can be purchased rather cheaply in pharmacies and health-food stores. Here are some do-it-yourself hair recipes. The first one is from La Coupe, Hair Salon in New York; the rest are recipes grandma told me.

Walnut Coloring Recipe:
For use to cover brown hair that is up to fifty percent gray. A safe, natural treatment using walnuts and henna.

1. Take walnut shells from 1 pound of walnuts and brown the shells, only, in a frying pan. Mix the browned shells with 1 quart of water and boil down, until the colored water is dark.

2. Remove the cooked shells and now add an equal amount of raw shells. Add another pint of water.

3. Boil down for one hour. The result: a dark brown liquid.

4. Take this liquid and mix it with a natural henna powder. (Purchase 1 packet natural henna at pharmacy or beauty-supply house.)

5. Apply this mixture to the head, then wrap head in Saran Wrap and sit under a portable dryer for at least twenty minutes.

6. Shampoo well.

Note: This natural rinse will add body and luster and a golden glow to graying or brown hair. It will slowly rinse out.

For Blondes Only:
To add refreshing highlights.

½ cup dried chamomile flowers
1 pint water

Boil the two ingredients for thirty minutes, strain and let cool. Pour the remaining liquid over freshly washed and dried hair, catching the remains in a basin. Repeat several times.

For Darkening Graying Hair:
This is a darkening application that you should use weekly for about five times, so that the hair gradually darkens. Reduce the frequency after, and as gray hair grows in, apply a bit more.

1 ounce rosemary herb
1 ounce sage leaves
1 pint water

Mix ingredients, put on stove and medium boil, then allow to simmer for half an hour. Strain. With cotton ball, massage throughout the hair to get a natural effect. Do at least once weekly for about five weeks.

For Damaged Hair:
Here is an excellent protein hair conditioner that you can use weekly, or if you have hair that has been damaged because of the use of strong chemicals or colors, you may need to use it at least every other time you wash your hair to get the best results.

¼ cup sesame seed or avocado oil
2 whole eggs
3 tablespoons castor oil

Mix the ingredients, apply to a dry head of hair, wrap in Saran Wrap or an old shower cap, and allow it to remain on the hair for at least thirty minutes. Shampoo gently and rinse with a vinegar rinse of 1/3 cup vinegar to 2 cups of water.

For Dandruff:
This may relieve the symptoms, but if they continue, you might have to see a dermatologist, as there are many forms of dandruff, including not enough oil being produced or dandruff flakes that are the result of a too oily scalp.

>   Shampoo
>   Vinegar rinse
>   2 effervescent antacid tablets
>   2/3 cup water

After shampooing your hair, use the antacid tablets (that you have dissolved in a cup of water) as a special soak rinse. Using cotton balls, blot the mixture all over the scalp, parting the hair in sections to get to all of the surface. Leave this solution on your scalp for at least fifteen minutes.
Now, rinse through with the vinegar rinse (1/3 cup vinegar to 2 cups of water) and make sure the antacid residue is all gone.

Hair Tips

- For dry split ends, you can singe the ends to seal them.
- Rosemary is an essential oil for the hair and can be purchased at many health-food stores, as well as herbalists. Add it to shampoos. It will make your hair smell nice too.
- Beer can be a great setting lotion. So can frothy egg whites, just as long as you brush well to remove the egg whites.
- Rub your hair section by section with a piece of silk. It will give your hair body and shine.
- After drinking your herbal teas, save all the leaves or tea bags and steep in hot water. Use this as a final rinse for your hair. It's a great conditioner. Some of the best herbs for the hair are dandelion, rosemary, violet leaves, parsley, peppermint leaf, elder blossoms, lemongrass, dulse, parsley, lavender, and rosemary. You'll find lots of herbal teas that contain these ingredients.

Natural Cleansing and Care for Your Face

The most common problems of the complexion—excessive oiliness or dryness, blackheads, whiteheads, and blemishes—are usually caused by disturbances to the skin's natural acid mantle (a complex mixture of many skin secretions that cover your body from head to toe) or the layer of dead skin cells that are sloughed off the body each day. Eliminating those disturbances will help you to keep your complexion as clear as it is meant to be.

In order to deep-clean the complexion, some method must be used to penetrate filled pores. If properly executed, there won't be any skin irritation. A soft natural bristle brush, or sturdy washcloth, or in some cases, a Loofa, can serve to create the proper friction for removing the dead cell layers without irritating the rest.

Following are some recipes and remedies for cleansing the skin; choose for your basic skin type.

For Normal Skin:
Papaya Mint Tea Treatment
This tea application can be a part of your weekly face scrub. Purchase tea bags through a health-food shop. To prepare, bring 2 cups of water to a boil, then place 2 papaya mint tea bags in the boiling pot of water. Allow tea to simmer, then steep the brew for a few minutes. Take a clean face cloth and dip into tea. Wring out and then apply to skin, just as long as it isn't burning hot. Avoid the eye area. The warm tea solution will help remove the accumulated dead cells from the skin. Continue rinsing face for at least ten minutes with cloth dipped in hot tea. If tea cools, reheat gently. If you have very sensitive skin or broken veins, use this treatment with extra caution.

For Excessively Oily Skin:
Yogurt Face Conditioner
This is an excellent premakeup applicator. Take 1

teaspoon of plain yogurt, smooth onto your face and neck until it disappears. Let it dry naturally. Then follow with your regular makeup application.

For Oily Skin:
Farina-Oatmeal Scrub
Ingredients: 1 cup uncooked oatmeal
             1 tablespoon farina (uncooked)

Place oatmeal in a blender and grind to a gritty powder. Add the farina and mix throughly. Store in a closed container for use as you need it.
To cleanse with this homemade scrub:

- Splash face with 7 handfuls of hot water to help dissolve greasy accumulations.
- Pick up a tablespoonful of the powder with wet fingers and gently scrub all over your face.
- Rinse well, with at least 10 handfuls of water.
- Pat dry, then follow with a vinegar rinse of 1 cup water to 1 tablespoon of vinegar.

For Dry Skin:
Sweet Butter and Whole Milk Cleanser
Melt a teaspoon of sweet butter and beat it into a few tablespoons of whole milk. Apply liberally to your skin. Use a lukewarm water wash to remove. Follow with a pat of cold water.

For Dry Skin:
Avocado Scrub
To remove dead cells, about once weekly take a ripe avocado half, mash or put it into a blender, then use as a facial mask by wiping it all over the face, using

fingers to tap and to press lightly. Allow the mixture to remain on for five minutes, then gently wash off with tap water.

For Problem Skin:
The Magic Mask Treatment

> 1 tablespoon oatmeal
> ½ teaspoonful cornmeal
> 1 egg white

Combine ingredients and apply to the face. Allow the mask to set, then remove by rubbing gently with your fingers until it flakes off. The friction of your fingers will help loosen and lift away surface blemishes.

For Oily Problem Skin:
Almond-Meal Cleanser
This one you can prepare ahead and keep by your sink for daily use.

> ½ cup almond meal
> ½ cup grated castile or vegetable protein soap
> ½ cup Indian cornmeal

Mix the ingredients together without adding any liquid. When you're ready to clean your face, dip into the container you keep the mixture in for just a tiny palmful. Add enough water to combine the dry ingredients and carefully rub into the skin. Be careful not to irritate sensitive tissue, but do create enough friction to cleanse and stimulate. Rinse off with tepid water and blot-dry. Follow with an apple-cider vinegar rinse of 1/4 cup vinegar, 3/4 cup water.

Being Your Own Beautician

Yes, it is also possible to have a fine complexion and never buy a pot of cream or bottle of lotion. Smooth, delicate, peaches and cream complexions existed long before man manufactured expensive cosmetics. By turning to simple preparations you can mix in your own kitchen, you can achieve the same results, and often better ones, than those promised on the label of that expensively packaged designer cream. All you need to know is that the removal of the tired, lifeless complexion requires discipline and good living habits, time and patience, and your caring enough about yourself to learn all you can about natural products that can help you.

The Good Night Night Cream
> 2 tablespoons cocoa butter
> 2 tablespoons lanolin
> ½ teaspoon honey
> 3 tablespoons almond oil
> 2 teaspoons rose water

Place the first 3 ingredients in a glass custard dish in a pan of hot water over a low flame. Stir the contents with a wooden spoon until they're melted and smooth. Remove the custard cup from the pan and add 2 teaspoons of rose water and 1/2 teaspoon honey. Cool the mixture and then beat until well blended. Pour the cream into a small container. Apply nightly for best results, on face and throat.

Lovely Lettuce Cream
>   1 cup lettuce
>   2 drops rose geranium oil or any flower oil
>   ½ cup lanolin

Wash the lettuce and cut it into fine strips. Heat the lanolin (which you'll have to purchase in an apothecary or pharmacy shop) in a nonmetallic container over boiling water until it liquefies. Add the lettuce and continue to heat a few moments longer. Remove from the heat and add the scent. Beat until cold and pack into small containers. The lettuce refines and refreshes the skin and the lanolin will add some nourishment.

Honey Toner
>   ¼ cup uncooked honey at room temperature

Pat the honey briskly over your face and neck. Allow it to remain on for about ten minutes while you relax. Then pat briskly once more before rinsing with warm water. That's all there is to it. A few more treatments will leave your skin with a soft feel.

Exhilarating Easy Facial
Beat 2 raw eggs, then paint them onto your face with a cotton ball. Allow to dry until your face feels stiff, then rinse well with warm water that has had a chamomile tea bag steeping in it.

Super Emollient Cream
>   1 ounce lanolin
>   ½ ounce almond oil
>   ½ ounce apricot kernel oil

Enough vitamin E capsules to supply 2,500 units per ounce

Melt the lanolin in a tiny pan, add the oils, and then pierce your vitamin E capsules with a sterilized needle and add to the mixture. Store in a jar with cover. Gently massage this cream into the area around your eyes and any place that is dry and sensitive, including your neck.

For Freckles and Age Spots

Grate 1 tablespoon of fresh horseradish into 2 tablespoons of buttermilk and let it sit for at least two hours before straining. Then apply to freckles or dark spots. Use daily for results.

For Sallow Skin:

1 oz. barley flour (purchase in health-food shop)
1 oz. blanched almonds
Honey

Pulverize the almonds and mix into the barley flour. Add just enough honey to make a smooth paste. Apply to your face and allow it to remain at least thirty minutes. Remove gently with warm water.

Skin Food Cream

2 mashed raw carrots
3 tablespoons wheat germ oil
1 teaspoon apple-cider vinegar
1 tablespoon honey

Beat ingredients together until well blended. Apply nightly after thoroughly cleansing the face. Allow this

cream to remain on all night, or if it gets messy, at
least until bedtime, which should give you an hour's
reading or TV time or relaxation before allowing your
face to hit the pillow.

For Distressed Skin:
> 1 tablespoon softened sweet butter
> 1 teaspoon egg yolk

Apply this creamy mixture to a clean face and neck
and allow it to remain on for a minimum of fifteen
minutes. Rinse off with warm water and splash an astringent mix of 1/2 juice of lemon to 1/4 cup of water
over your face as the final rinse.

For Chafed or Chapped Hands:
> 2 egg yolks
> 2 tablespoons oil of sweet almond
> 1 tablespoon rose water
> 1 pair old white kid gloves

Beat the egg yolks until they are a bright yellow.
Whip in the almond oil and blend well with the rose
water. Line the gloves with this penetrating mixture,
then slip your hands inside and wear this all night if
you can. By the way, leather is preferable to cotton
since the cotton would only absorb the lotion. Your
hands will more easily absorb the rich oils and protein
from the eggs when encased in the kid.

Suntan Lotion for Oily and Tan Skin:
This homemade suntanning lotion is good for any
skin that doesn't sunburn or burn easily. If you have
sensitive skin, don't use it, but seek a product with a

good PABA sun blocker. This recipe, spread on oily or tan skin, will spread beautifully and will give you an all-over tan.

> ¾ cup water
> ¼ cup lanolin
> 3 tea bags
> ¼ cup sesame oil

First, heat the water to boiling and soak the tea bags for at least twenty minutes, squeezing them occasionally to get the most out of them. Remove the bags and you should have a good 1/2 cup of quadruple-strength tea. (Any type of tea will do, it needn't be herbal.)

In another medium-size enamel pot, measure out the lanolin and sesame oil, and heat them gently over boiling water. As soon as the oils are melted together, take them off the hot water and very slowly add the half-cup of strong tea, beating constantly with your electric mixer on medium setting. (If you notice some of the tea floating on top of the oil, stop until the tea is absorbed, then begin to slowly pour again.) Continue this process until all the tea is used.

When all the tea has been added, increase your beater speed to high and whip the cream for five minutes. You've now made yourself a cup of coffee-colored cream that is actually water repellent and is excellent for sunbathing and swimming.

Note: You can purchase PABA tablets at the vitamin/health food store and pulverize at least 10 to 20 of them, to get at least a strength equal to 500 units, and add it into the cream to create a far more effective sun-blocking agent. This is a must if you

have fair skin and want to protect it from the sun yet
want to do up your own sunning lotion.

Quick Repairs and Instant Answers

What about emergencies? What should you do when
you have just run out of a lipstick, or perhaps you
don't have time to get a manicure done, or your hair is
oily and you have just been invited out to a special
place? Well, there are little quickie tips you can learn
to help yourself find an alternative way of handling
just about any crisis, whether it's a broken fingernail
or a lost rouge. Here are some helpers.

INSTANT SHAMPOO: When there's no time to shampoo
your hair but it looks limp and oily, then dust it with
baby powder or powdered orrisroot (which you'll find
at the drugstore). Rub the powder through the hair
for a few minutes, then brush it out vigorously, until
your hair shines.

Another trick: Cover your hairbrush with cheesecloth that you have sprayed with your favorite cologne. Then brush through. The dust and dirt will
cling to the cloth and your hair will be temporarily
clean.

BROKEN FINGERNAIL: When you tear or break a nail
and can't do a whole manicure, you can patch up one
nail quickly. First, remove the polish to inspect the
damage. Then cut out a piece of fine tissue paper to
fit the missing part, then place a coat of clear sealer on
the paper as you affix it to your nail. Use the sealer

on top of the patch and around it. Now add polish. By the way, you can also take some glue and use it as a temporary fixative. However, the Crazy Glue that works best takes special care, as it can adversely affect the skin around it.

QUICK ASTRINGENT: If you need to wash the oil or grime from your face, the cheapest and best astringent is witch hazel. Soak some cotton balls in it and use it to wipe your face as you need them. To carry dampened cotton balls, find an empty pill container and pack the witch hazel–soaked balls into the container. Carry in your handbag for freshening up later.

SUNBURN: Despite all warnings, if you're still suffering from staying out too long in the sun and your face or body is red, try a soothing bath in tepid water with a small box of bicarbonate of soda. Or soak in a bath of tepid water and two cups of cider vinegar. For a serious burn, any fever, or swelling, do see a doctor. And next time, be sure to wear a sun-blocking agent.

PUFFY EYES: Cut a fresh potato into slices and use one on each eyelid. Lie back and give yourself at least ten minutes. Also soaking cotton pads in warm witch hazel can help. Watch the salt in your diet: it often is the cause of puffy eyelids and swollen ankles.

SHINE ON: A dab of petroleum jelly can serve as many a makeup substitute. For instance, it will brighten your eyes when there's no eye shadow handy. Use on your eyelashes nightly for lubrication, and if you haven't any mascara handy, then use instead. It will make your lashes shine and darken them slightly. Lipstick missing? Of course you can use some petroleum jelly as gloss. And, if you're out of blusher, a dot of lipstick on each cheek, then a dab of jelly, and all you have to do is blend well.

Mosquito Bite: Believe it or not, garlic will work wonders. Just take one clove, pulverize, and place on whatever spot itches you, and presto, it will be gone. They say onion works too.

CHAPTER IX

Special Makeup Situations

Covering Up Scars and Blemishes

There are certain times of the month, often connected with the menstrual cycle, when blemishes can be a problem. Is there a convenient way to cover up? Then, there are those other marks that are not so temporary—like red splotches, spidery red lines, birthmarks, moles, and such that may distort or disturb your smooth-as-a-peach-pretty look. Again, you'll want to camouflage most skin blemishes so that when applying your makeup it will result in an even foundation, a good start, and a smooth-as-silk appearance.

Television is a good setting in which to point out some professional tips. We asked a real pro, makeup artist Carmen Gebbia, who has long been with the Westinghouse Broadcasting Network, for advice on how he covers up scars and blemishes on guests who must appear before the camera.

"There is a makeup called Covermark, made by Lydia O'Leary, that has been around for years, and has been used by stage and television actors and actresses. I use it to cover up black- and prune-color marks, other discolorations and scars," says Gebbia. He also suggests that you investigate getting a makeup like a Max Factor pancake if you can't find Lydia O'Leary Covermark in your locale; pancake makeup is thick and will also do the job well.

The method that works best in camouflaging blemishes, offers Gebbia, is by patting or stippling it on the blemish, *not* by rubbing. Then add a powder that blends in with the shade of pancake makeup. Again, pat, and don't rub the powder over your face.

By the way, Carmen Gebbia suggests using petroleum jelly as an inexpensive moisturizer. Merely wet the hands and apply lightly over the drier areas of your face for a quiet sheen.

Between the Lines

As we age, we wrinkle and there's little that we can do to prevent them, nor the sagging jowl lines, the pouches, the fine lines around the eyes, all part of the eventual aging process. The soft tissues of the skin naturally lose their elasticity and begin to sag. By being extremely cautious about sun exposure, by eating healthful foods, by sleeping enough, and by using the proper skin-treatment products to continually nourish the skin, we can stave off premature aging signals and even minimize the deleterious effects upon the skin.

Wrinkles reflect your general health, age, genes, lifetime exposure to sun and wind, skin elasticity, and weight throughout your life. If you're wrinkling, approaching forty or beyond, and are unhappy about some of the features that seem to be showing signs of deterioration—like a general laxity of the tissues about your mouth and jawline, than perhaps you should consider cosmetic surgery. Today it is becoming a rather common choice, and far more affordable and acceptable for women.

What Is Plastic Surgery?

It is a specialty of medicine that seeks to heal and restore patients with injury, disfigurement, or scarring resulting from accidents, disease, or birth defects. It includes both aesthetic or cosmetic surgery to correct or recontour facial and bodily features that are not pleasing. The word *plastic*, from the Greek, actually means molding, or giving form, and does not refer to synthetic plastic materials.

Aesthetic surgery, or cosmetic, can correct problems of the face, neck, and abdomen, including the nose, eyes, ear, chin, breasts, arms, and thighs. From burns to acne-pitted scars to benign and malignant tumors, you may seek redress through the technical assistance of a plastic surgeon.

Consult your family physician, call your local county medical society, ask your local teaching or first-class community hospital, or write to: American Society of Plastic and Reconstructive Surgeons, Inc., 29 East Madison, Suite 800, Chicago, Illinois 60602, for the names of qualified plastic surgeons in your area.

Makeup and Care After Surgery

When your surgeon says it is safe, and only then, you may reapply makeup to the areas that have been operated upon. Initially after surgery, care should be carefully instructed by your doctor. Your face, and whatever particular area upon it that has been surgically involved, should be properly protected through the initial healing process. Usually an antiseptic wash like Betadine is prescribed. You may use this instead of ordinary soap for washing.

It is important to note here that the effects of the surgery will be much longer lasting if you take care of your skin in a proper manner. This means staying out of the sun and wind, not subjecting your skin to harsh abuse. If you spent a great deal of money on a fur coat, you would take great care of it. It's surprising how many women will spend money on cosmetic surgery and then ignore taking aftercare.

Do look for products that are gentle, that are allergy-tested and demonstrated to have hypo-allergic tendencies. After, the proper use of cosmetics can enhance the total look, and give you a new glow.

Special Dos

After a face-lift or eyelid surgery, gently wash the areas after the third day, and pat dry. Do keep some cold moist soaks in the refrigerator to use over your eyes.

Initially there will be swelling wherever there has been cutting and suturing. It's the normal step in the body healing itself. As for disguising black and blue marks in the early postoperative period, there are very good skin-care products that are gentle and can be used effectively. (Try Lydia O'Leary's cover-up or some pancake makeup.) You can pat some liquid makeup over the area that is discolored and gently blend.

If you have had work done on your nose, then you can use makeup right after the splint is removed, since any incisions are inside. However, gently patting on makeup and avoiding any pressure on the areas in question is important, including using a light eyeglass frame for postnasal surgery and taping it above the bridge of the nose in such a manner that the frames are not resting on the nose itself.

Most doctors recommend a pH-balanced soap, one that should be adjusted for the type of skin, from too dry, too oily, or normal. You'll find a wealth of products on the market, so pick and choose carefully.

Special Don'ts

Iridescent makeup usually irritates and should not be used near incisions or scars to avoid any problems. There are enough eye shadows, rouges, and powders without the iridescent ingredients to give you a wide choice of colors, so forgo their use after surgery.

Don't go out without applying liberal doses of sunblocking cream during the sunny part of each day. Do make sure that you wear a hat to add shadows and protection whenever your face is exposed to the sun.

Certain types of deep cleansing facials are damaging and can even speed the aging process by overmanipulation of the skin. Certainly, for the first six months after cosmetic surgery of the face, you're better off without a professional facial. You'll find many natural and easy masks within this guide that you can safely use postoperatively.

CHAPTER X

Free Information, Material, and Services

Beauty Bag

To put on a new face, to take the best care of your hair, your skin, and your body, and to do it practically, at money-saving, bargain-basement ways—you'll need patience, time, and the fortitude to ask questions when you need to. You'll also want to find out the best possible places to shop and to learn.

With so many fantastic beauty products to choose from and with such a wide range of prices, it is up to you to become responsible and to learn how to become an aware consumer. This book will give you the tips and hints and many product mentions. The rest is up to you. For the American cosmetics business is ever changing—there are constant breakthroughs in products, in colors, and in manufacturers. The cream you use today can be eliminated tomorrow. And the twenty-five-dollar version you wish you could own but don't want to spend that much for, just might be found in the discount store next season.

Of course, you can and should follow the label directions carefully. They are there to protect you. And you should be wise about *all* the ingredients, because the regulations that govern ingredient labeling are also there to provide you with protection. If you find the words confusing, then by all means go to the library and take out a book on the subject—there are many to help you, like *Cosmetics: What the Ads Don't Tell You* by Carol Ann Rinzler (Thomas Y. Crowell Company, 1977) and *The Buyer's Guide to Cosmetics* by Pat Boughton and Martha Ellen Hughes (Random House, 1981). And of course there are excellent consumer-oriented magazines.

Miss-Mistakes

Don't let that title apply to you. First, never assume a product will look the same on you as it does on a friend or in the package. Test and test some more. For instance, a lipstick always looks different on the lips than it does when one tests it on the back of the hand. After all, the color is seen in relation to your rouge, eye, and hair color; so do test lipstick on your lips for foolproof wearing. And don't buy anything just because it looks great on the model in that magazine. It just may not work for you. And last but not least, don't let any makeup saleslady nor hairdresser tell you what you should be wearing. If you just hate red hair and blue eye shadow and that's what they're recommending, follow your own basic nature. Intuition works best. For if you don't feel pretty in globs of makeup, then the best and most professional advice won't work. You should feel comfortable in the wearing.

Complaint Department

What to do when something goes wrong? Like the lipstick breaks and you're sure it was weak; after all it happened the first time you applied it? Worse, you find a fly in the cream? Well, you can write a letter to the product manager or the marketing director of the company in question and say just what didn't please you about the product, what happened, and why. You might not get your money back, but you're more than likely going to get a free product. Companies have customer-relations policies and the policy is in your favor.

It's your money. If you feel you have a legitimate complaint about the hair dye or the cologne or the result you get with the cream you have purchased, write and let the manufacturer know how you, the consumer, feel. Of course, save your sales slips—this may help and you can also bring the product back to the store. Most reputable stores will give you an immediate adjustment or replacement. Better still, ask for your money back if the product doesn't do what the ad or package promises.

If you're writing to the manufacturer, an address is important. Some also offer consumers toll-free WATS numbers, so that if you have a question on how to use a certain product, or where to purchase it in your area, you'll find an immediate response is possible. Following is a partial list of many of the manufacturers who have products you're more than likely to purchase in the five and dime, discount, and chain stores.

Aziza Eye Cosmetics
33 Benedict Place
Greenwich, Connecticut
06830

Bonne Bell, Inc.
18519 Detroit Avenue
Lakewood, Ohio 44107

John H. Breck, Inc.
Berdan Avenue
Wayne, New Jersey 07470

Chap Stick Company
1000 Robins Road
Lynchburg, Virginia
24505

Chesebrough-Pond's Inc.
33 Benedict Place
Greenwich, Connecticut
06830

Clairol, Inc.
345 Park Avenue
New York, New York
10022
Toll-free number:
(800) 223-5800

Coty, Div. of Pfizer, Inc.
235 East 42nd St.
New York, New York
10017

Helene Curtis Industries,
Inc.
4401 West North Avenue
Chicago, Illinois 60639

Max Factor & Co.
1655 N. McCadden Place
Hollywood, California
90028

Fashion Fair
820 South Michigan
Avenue
Chicago, Illinois 60605

Johnson & Johnson
Baby Products Company
501 George Street
New Brunswick,
New Jersey 08903

The Nestle-LeMur
Company
902 Broadway
New York, New York
10010

Noxell Corporation
11050 York Road
Baltimore, Maryland
21203

Plough, Inc. (Maybelline)
303 Jackson Avenue
Memphis, Tennessee
38151

Revlon, Inc.
767 Fifth Avenue
New York, New York
10022

Roux Laboratories, Inc.
Prudential Building
Jacksonville, Florida
32207

Scholl, Inc.
213 W. Schiller Street
Chicago, Illinois 60610

Tussy Cosmetics, Inc.
Lehn & Fink Products Co.
225 Summit Avenue
Montvale, New Jersey
07645

The Wella Corporation
524 Grand Avenue
Englewood, New Jersey
07631

Cheap Tricks

There are free booklets, instructions, samples, and charts that you'll find available from manufacturers and foundations. Some of the items will change, so that the present Bonne Bell booklet on diet and exercise, an excellent fifty-two-page guide, may be updated or not in print, but it certainly doesn't hurt to ask. All you have to do is to write to any of the above manufacturers asking for any informational guides they have available. More than likely you'll be deluged with booklets loaded with tips. Johnson & Johnson, for instance, produces at least a dozen excellent booklets for consumers that give you a variety of money-saving methods of using their products.

For a list of free booklets on such subjects as "What Every Woman Should Know About High Blood Pressure," "Nutrition, Food at Work for You," you can write to one great source that lists more than two hundred consumer publications from the federal government in one catalog. Just write to "Catalog." c/o Consumer Information Center, Dept. 48, Pueblo, Colorado 81009.

Free For All . . .

Here, some good information on skin and hair care available for free or for the price of postage:

For years Rachel Perry has been distributing a unique line of skin-care products in health-food stores around the country. Some of them are excellent, like Lemon-Mint Astringent and Violet-Rose Skin Toner. If you would like to know about her skin-care philosophy and program, write for Rachel Perry's helpful booklet entitled *For the Skin of Your Life.* This twelve-page booklet offers information about her line of special products for different skin types. Send a self-addressed, stamped, legal-size envelope along with your request to: Rachel Perry, 8137 Remmet Avenue, Dept. BD, Canoga Park, California 91304.

Do you know what kind of roller to use to give your hair extra fullness? How about what brush is best for detangling extra-thick hair? Or how to put the finishing touch on a soft and full hairstyle? To find out all the answers to these questions and more, send for *Goody's Styling Guide.* It shows you exactly what type of combs, brushes, perm rods, and rollers you'll need to achieve each look. Send fifty cents to: Goody Products, Inc., P. O. Box 450, Little Falls, New Jersey 07424. Allow 6–8 weeks for delivery.

Witch hazel has many medicinal properties as well as being an effective beauty aid. For the price of postage you can obtain two booklets that describe the many uses of witch hazel. *Be Beautiful from Head to Toe* contains thirty beauty tips, including how to reduce frown lines and make an oily skin mask and instant shampoo. *The Birth of Witch Hazel* tells how this remarkable lotion was discovered and its many health uses. Send a request for these two booklets, by name, and a self-addressed, stamped envelope to: The E. E. Dickinson Company, 40-46 North Main Street, Essex, Connecticut 06426.

Being There: Take a Tour

Many companies offer you tours of their premises, where you'll see those giant vats that are filled with reds and pinks and blues and plums, liquids bubbling over and ready to fill those jars that line the shelves of drugstores, cosmetic counters, and discount outlets. You might even be able to arrange a tour for your club—if you belong to a women's bridge, gardening, or social club and want to see just how the plants operate, write asking for a tour to the public relations department of the cosmetics manufacturer you are interested in viewing.

Bonne Bell knows how curious women are. They'll take consumers regularly through their plant and show how a product like their Ten-O-Six lotion is developed. You can visit the lab, talk to the real chemists who have created the formula, and you can also get answers to any beauty questions you may have. (Their address is listed within this chapter.)

Getting Freebies

Freebies are the popular term for sample sizes, handouts for promotional purposes, like product tie-ins, and a totally free haircut, coloring, or makeup application. How? Simple. Just phone up your local chain stores, the giants in the beauty industry, like Seligman & Latz and Glemby. They have local shops within department stores all over the country; all you need is to look in your local directory for the name, and spend some time finding out in which stores near you the chain is located. You might also live in a town that has a Clairol or other leading hair-color manufacturer. Here, too, volunteers are sought out for testing. Most beauty and hairdressing schools give free facials and haircuts, perms and color too. Look them up in the Yellow Pages. Often ads are taken in newspapers asking for models. Read the papers, where you'll find announcements of guest makeup artists demonstrating a line of beauty makeup and products, hair-cutting demonstrations, new exercise clinics with sample lessons, and so on.

The idea: If you'll take advantage of attending seminars in stores (where, often, for the price of admission you get a grab bag of makeup samples) ; if you'll go to the large department store's cosmetics counter when a guest makeup artist has been announced, then you can get a free makeup lesson and application. And by asserting yourself and phoning the giant chains, where often new hairdressers are trained after hours, and volunteer models are sorely needed, you can get anything from a free hair coloring, to hair cutting, to conditioning, to the whole works.

From makeup clinics to tester units to on-the-spot demonstrations where you get a free application, there are many ways to save money, get fresh hints and help and even products and services without paying anything at all.

Beauty-Supply Houses

Giant shampoo sizes that will last you and the family a whole year. Dryers. Rollers. Hairbrushes. Dyes and bleaches. Clips by the ton. You name it and more than likely you'll find it cheaper at your local beauty-supply store. Sure, they're really there to service hairdressers, but they will offer consumers discounts—sometimes as much as thirty percent off.

So do look up your nearest shop under "Beauty Supplies" and take a friend along—you might be able to save even more if the two of you can agree on one hair spray or type of hair conditioner and if you order more than a dozen, well, the price is often even less. Or, organize a beauty products buyer's club in your neighborhood and you may well be able to purchase at wholesale prices.

Other Books to Help You

This guide will give you a start in learning how to make up and care for yourself better and cheaper. Others can give you supplementary information on certain subjects. Following is a list of some books that can give you more facts and inspiration:

The Medically Based No-Nonsense Beauty Book by Deborah Chase
  (Pocket Books, $1.95)

How to Cut Your Own Hair or Anybody Else's by Bob Bent
  (Quality Paperback, $4.95)

A Consumer's Dictionary of Cosmetic Ingredients by Ruth Winter
  (Crown, $3.95)

Free: *How to Achieve A Dancer's Body*
  Write: Capezio Dance, 543 West 43rd Street, New York, New York 10036

Free: *Question & Answer Booklet on Plastic Surgery*
  Write: American Society of Plastic and Reconstructive Surgeons, Inc., 29 East Madison, Suite 800, Chicago, Illinois 60602

Here's Egg on Your Face by Beatrice Traven (natural cosmetics)
  (Pocket Books, about $1.95)

Secrets of Health & Beauty by Linda Clark
    (Pyramid, about $1.75)

How to Keep Slender and Fit After Thirty by Bonnie
    Prudden
    (Pocket Books, $1.25)

New Age Training for Fitness and Health by Dyveke
    Spino
    (Grove Press, $12.50)

Smooth as Silk by Judi McMahon (a guide to super-
    fluous hair removal)
    (Hawthorn/Dutton Books, $3.95)

A Year of Beauty and Exercise for the Pregnant Woman
    by Judi McMahon
    (Lippincoff/Crowell, $12.95)

Free: Booklet explaining the free Overeaters Anony-
    mous program. Send a stamped self-addressed en-
    velope with 20¢ for booklet to:
    Overeaters Anonymous
    World Service Office
    3730 Motor Avenue
    Los Angeles, California 90034

Total Beauty Catalog by K. T. Maclay
    (Coward, McCann & Geoghegan, Inc., $7.95)[1]

Note: Some of the books are available at the discount
bookshop. Better still, go to your library and borrow
them.